CHILD ABUSE
AND
DELINQUENCY

D1597630

Suman Kakar

University Press of America, Inc.
Lanham • New York • London

Copyright © 1996 by
University Press of America,® Inc.
4720 Boston Way
Lanham, Maryland 20706

3 Henrietta Street
London, WC2E 8LU England

Library of Congress Cataloging-in-Publication Data

Kakar, Suman.
Child abuse and delinquency / Suman Kakar.
p.   cm.
Includes bibliographical references and index.
1. Child abuse--United States--Research. 2. Juvenile delinquency--
United States--Research. I. Title.
HV6626.52.K34   1996   364.3'6'0973--dc20   96-15004 CIP

ISBN 0-7618-0368-8 (cloth: alk. ppr.)
ISBN 0-7618-0369-6 (pbk: alk. ppr.)

♾ The paper used in this publication meets the minimum
requirements of American National Standard for information
Sciences—Permanence of Paper for Printed Library Materials,
ANSI Z39.48—1984

This book is dedicated to my family:

Especially to
my parents: Shanti Devi and Diwan Chand Kakkar, who gave me
life, love, opportunity, and encouragement to strive for excellence;
my grandparents: Parsini Devi and Udho Ram Kakkar, whose
outlook and whose pride and trust in me empowered me to take a
stand, make a difference, and be counted; my sons: Pariskshat
Sirpal and Sanjeev Sirpal whose love, patience, understanding,
and gracious eagerness to help were constant source of
encouragement.

To my mentors at the University of Florida
and the Department of Sociology,
Joe R. Feagin and Hernan Vera whose outlook on life, and
tremendous faith in   me changed my life completely.

And to all those who are involved in helping the abused and
delinquent children through research and service

Contents

List of Figures

List of Tables

ACKNOWLEDGMENTS

I wish to express my thanks and deep appreciation to colleagues, professional associates, and friends who contributed to this book. Special thanks are due to Hernan Vera and Joe Feagin who were among the first to see the importance of the book on relationship between child abuse and delinquency. Their mentor ship, editorial suggestions, constant encouragement, and moral support helped bring this project to completion. I also want to thank Michelle Harrison and Helen Hudson, editors at the University Press of America for their editorial comments. I am grateful to my friend and colleague, Miriam Potocky, Ph.D., School of Social Work, who read several versions of this book with enthusiasm and excitement and provided astute comments.

I would like to express my special thanks and appreciation to my colleagues at the Florida International University who supported me as I initiated and developed this project: Mark Rosenberg, Ph.D. Dean , College of Urban and Public Affairs; Donald Klinger, Ph.D., Associate Dean, College of Urban and Public Affairs; David Bergwall, Ph.D., School of Policy and Management; Fred. Newman, Ph.D., Associate Professor, Health Services Administration;   Milan Dluhy, Ph.D., Institute of Government; Howrd Frank, Ph.D., Coordinator, Public Administration, School of Policy and Management; Clinton Terry, Ph.D., Associate Professor, Criminal Justice; and Ray Surrette, Ph.D. Professor, Criminal Justice. I wish to thank Ruth Pacheco, Programmer Analyst for being patient and helping me with her computer expertise and office. I also thank my graduate and undergraduate students for their interest and enthusiastic participation in discussions of child abuse and delinquency in lecture classes, seminars, and directed research.

I also want to thank Ronald Clarke, Ph.. D., Dean, School of Criminal Justice, Rutgers University and Mangai Natrajan, Ph. D., Department of Sociology, John Jay College of Criminal Justice for their helpful advice, good cheer, and laughter.

I express my thanks to Mr. Robert Brake, Mr. David West, and the staff of the Children, Youth, and Families department of the Department of Health and Rehabilitative Services in Florida, District Three. I am very grateful for their help, support, time, patience, and understanding.

My most special thanks go to my sons, Parikshat and Sanjeev Sirpal for being sources of endless love, strength, patience, understanding, and encouragement.

Chapter 1

Child Abuse An Introduction

Child abuse and delinquency are some of the most critical social problems facing contemporary U.S. society. Daily newspaper and television stories send us disheartening reminders that children are brutally abused, neglected, molested, and sometimes even killed by the very people who are entrusted with their care and protection. Millions of children are abandoned, denied an ooportunity to grow up in a nurturing environment - essential for normal growth - and forced into situations that leave them no option but do whatever is necessary for survival. The same sources also provide us with chilling accounts of brutal acts of violence committed by juveniles against family as well as non-family members. In 1992, juveniles accounted for 13 percent of all violent crimes reported to law enforcement agencies and 18 percent of all violent crime arrests. According to the Federal Bureau of Investigation (1992), the rate of violent crime by juveniles, defined as people from 10 to 17 years of age, increased more than 25 percent in the last decade.

Child rearing techniques and the environment in which children are brought up is thought to have lasting effects on children. This environment is known to help children learn and internalize social and legal norms of the society. It influences their behavior, decision making process, and thinking pattern. It is agreed upon by the experts and general public alike that children learn through imitation. Observing adults' behavior helps them develop their personalities, philosophies, and outlook on life. Thus, it is not a surprise that we find early childhood victimization distorting child's thinking patterns. It is not a surprise that abused children are more likely to engage in abusive and delinquent behavior. A 17th century English philanthropist articulates the relationship between child rearing and delinquent acts very effectively. He writes:

. . . Let any man that hath occasion either to walk or ride through the Outskirts of this City (where mostly our poor people inhabit) tell but what he hath seen of the Rudeness of young children, who for want of better education and employment, shall sometimes be found by whole companies at play, where they shall wrangle and cheat one another, and upon the least provocation swear and fight for a farthing, or else they shall be found whipping of horses, by reasons of which, they sometimes cast their riders to the hazard or loss of their lives or limbs or else they shall be throwing dirt or stones into coaches . . . . They have been generally so much neglected, that they have neither been taught their duties towards God or man.

When a trusted and depended-upon adult is actively inflicting pain on the child, s/he is forced into confusing, traumatic, and crisis-like situations. S/he not only must cope with pain and abuse but also contend with the fact that the persons inflicting that pain are the people who should be loving and protecting her/him. Child abuse violates the child's view of the world as a benevolent, ordered, predictable, and safe place, impairs their social and moral judgements, and forces them to be thinking about survival at all costs, at an early and tender age. Although the association between a history of child abuse and youth who commit delinquent acts has not been definitively established, there is considerable evidence pointing to the fact that the effects of early childhood victimization are severe and persistent. Experts and the general public seem to agree that our rearing styles have implications for children's subsequent behavior and the children growing up in an abusive environment are more likely to engage in delinquent activities as compared to children growing up in nurturing environment. Steele (1976) presents this view adequately when he comments, "If one's early life was unfortunately beset by neglect and abuse, then one is likely to repeat it . . ." Although most abused children do not grow up to be abusive, the risk of them being so is much greater than if they had not been abused.

Over the last twenty-five years child abuse has emerged as a central theme in efforts to understand a wide variety of problems, including delinquency. The accumulating body of research on the risk of delinquency among the abused children provides differing views on the magnitude of the abuse-delinquency relationship.

Many scholars (Curtis, 1963; Garbarino, 1976; Garbarino 1989; Kratcoski, 1982, 1985; Garbarino and Plantz, 1986; Kaufman and Zigler, 1987; Kaufman and Cicchetti, 1989; Garbarino and Gilliam, 1980; Straus et al. 1980; Widom, 1989a, 1989b, and 1989c; Garbarino, 1990) have hypothesized that children who are victims of abuse during the early years of their lives are more likely to victimize family as well as non-family members, particularly through violent acts. Phrases like "cycle of violence" and "intergenerational transmission of violence" are liberally used in the criminology and child abuse literatures to explain the association between child abuse, subsequent delinquency, and crime. Several deficits and problems in juveniles' and adults' lives have been hypothesized to have some association with the childhood experience of abuse.

Researchers predict that the aftermath of abuse is likely to include violence, social maladjustment, and multifarious other developmental problems (Oliver and Taylor, 1971; Martin 1976; Alfaro, 1981; Mouzakitis, 1981; Perry et al. 1983; Lewis et al. 1989). The notion that children who experience abuse will grow up to have deficits and abuse others, makes common sense. It is not difficult to envision the cataclysmic effect, the experience of abuse and neglect may have on children. Children, powerless individuals, who look up to their parents or their adult caretakers for care, protection, guidance, and support are hit, injured, sexually molested, subjected to pain and suffering, neglected, or emotionally abused. This breach of trust at an early age, when a child's mind is tender and impressionable, may have disastrous and long-lasting effects. The traumatic experiences of abuse by persons who are supposed to love and nurture the children may have several negative long-term effects. Abused children are likely to develop a fixed perception of the world and internalize their experiences as appropriate ways of behaving toward others.

Although these ideas have intuitive appeal, the path from the experience of child abuse to the acts of delinquency may not be as direct as is usually assumed. Many intervening events during an individual's life may mitigate or exacerbate the effects of abuse (Widom, 1989a).

Since the seminal investigation by Elmer and Gregg (1967) suggested severe and pervasive psychosocial effects of abuse on children, extensive research has been conducted to explore the sequelae of abuse. These studies suggest that the effects of abuse are felt in numerous ways, such as neurological functioning, intellectual functioning, social cognition, physical and emotional injury, and low self-esteem.

The consequences of abuse are many and varied, and delinquency is only one of the many possible social, social-psychological, and behavioral consequences of abuse (Zingraff et al. 1993). The adverse impact of abuse on children as they grow up has been documented by several researchers (e.g., Ammerman and Hersen, 1990; Cicchetti and Carlson, 1989; Daro, 1988; Justice and Justice, 1976; Azar et al., 1988; Conway and Hensen,

1989; Erickson et al., 1989; Widom, 1989a; Farrington, 1978; Carlson et al., 1989). Also a variety of deficits and dysfunctions, including insecure attachment formation (Egeland and Sroufe, 1981a; Crittenden, 1988), depression (Kazdin et al., 1985), anxiety (Green, 1978), behavior problems (McCord, 1983; Eyeberg and Ross, 1978), poor peer relations (Boshua and Twentyman, 1984), academic underachievement (Morgan, 1987), neuropsychological deficits (Tarter et al., 1984), and intellectual deficits (Hoffman-Plotkin and Twentyman, 1984) have been attributed to the childhood experiences.

Researchers in this area have been interested in an extremely broad range of concerns and questions. For example, from an epidemiological approach, the incidence and prevalence of abuse and its risk factors have been identified (Gelles, 1973; Gelles and Straus, 1987; Finkelhor and Hotalling, 1984). Other researchers have examined the characteristics of the perpetrators and the victims (Ainsworth and Wittig, 1969; Cicchetti, 1984; Cicchetti and Sroufe 1976; Loeber and Dishion, 1983; Wolfe 1985), the impact of abuse on the victim (Silver et al. 1969; Olweus, 1980; Main and George, 1985; Aber and Allen, 1987; Straker and Jacobson, 1981; Dean et al., 1986; Egeland, Sroufe, and Erickson, 1983), the intergenerational transmission of abuse, or the association between abuse and delinquency (Wolfe and Moske, 1983; Widom, 1989c; Bolton et al. 1977; McCord, 1983). Still other scholars have investigated the etiology of abuse -- the micro- and macro-social conditions surrounding the occurrence of abuse (Crittenden, 1985; Starr et al., 1990; Egeland and Brunnquell, 1979; Kotelchuck, 1982; Starr, 1979). Other scholars have scrutinized intervention and prevention strategies to assess the effectiveness of prevention and intervention programs (Besharov, 1983, 1984; Alvy, 1975; Otto and Melton, 1991); and some other researchers have proposed identifying the intervening variables in order to understand the factors and dynamics that lead to resiliency in the face of adversity (Eyberg and Ross, 1978; Gelles, 1980). Among these suggestions is the repeated claim that there is a significant relationship between abuse and neglect and later delinquent behavior among juveniles (Jenkins, 1968; Kratcoski, 1982; Lewis et al., 1979, 1985).

In spite of the voluminous research in this area, very few of these studies are considered methodologically sound. In fact, some researchers have questioned the findings of many studies. Gil, in 1973, described the existing research as unsystematic, fragmented, and distorted. Spinetta and Rigler (1972) stated that there are very few well- designed studies in child abuse and the most of them are just "professional opinions" on the subject.

Today, more than twenty years after these assertions were made, the research in this area has improved a great deal but still appears to be afflicted by some problem and most research seems to have limitations in one area or the other. The most common limitations of the earlier studies are felt in the research designs and methodologies, for example, no general definition (Aber and Zigler, 1981; Aber et al. 1984), poorly defined dependent and independent variables, confounding variables (Cicchetti and Rizley, 1981; Conway and Hensen, 1989), inadequate and/or biased sampling, no control groups (Widom, 1989), the use of inappropriate measures of unknown or inadequate reliability and validity, the inappropriate inferences and interpretations, and the lack of theoretical frameworks (Plotkin et al., 1981; Mash and Wolfe, 1991).

Thus, the state of the research in this area tells us that our knowledge of the relationship between abuse and delinquency is incomplete. Some studies assert a very significant relationship while others claim a modest one. Still other studies assert that no association exists between abuse and delinquency. Clearly, there is need for studies that are methodologically sound to examine the association between child abuse and the later delinquency from a sociological perspective.

This research examines the relationship between child abuse and delinquency using a quasi-experimental, longitudinal prospective design. In particular, this research seeks to address four specific questions: (a) Are abused children referred more for delinquent behavior as compared with non-abused children? (b) How significant are the differences in delinquency referral rates between abused and non-abused subjects? (b) Do these differences vary by racial group, age, and gender? © Do the outcomes differ by the severity of abuse?

The significance of studying the relationship between child abuse and delinquency from a sociological perspective lies in the fact that social norms, practices, and policies play a pivotal role in the way children are brought up. We cannot blame child abuse for all the problems our youth have today unless that really is the case. We need to examine other sociological factors that may be compounding the effects of abuse. Some of the previous studies that claim a strong relationship between child abuse and subsequent problems have limitations that caution us against generalizing and drawing conclusions from them. If we are to solve the problem we need to know what the magnitude of the problem is. For prevention and intervention programs to be effective and to develop policies for the protection and benefit of children, youth, and families, it is of absolute importance that we study this relationship carefully rather than beginning with the assumption that abuse is the direct cause of delinquency. Steele (1976) presents this argument very eloquently:

... we do believe that how we bring up our children has a most profound effect upon how our society is behaving and how we deal with each other as human beings. (pp. 291).

The main purpose of this research is to determine the degree to which delinquency is present in a selected sample of abused children and compare this presence with a matched control group's degree of involvement in delinquency.

The specific objectives of this research are as follows:

1.   To determine whether or not the abused children are referred more for delinquency than the non-abused.
2.   To determine whether the prevalence of delinquency varies by gender, racial group, or age.
3.   To assess one of the conditions, such as the severity of abuse, under which abuse is most likely to contribute to the subsequent delinquent behavior.

To address these questions, data were gathered on 477 abuse cases substantiated between January 1988 and December 1990 by District Three of the Florida Protective Services System's department of Children, Youth, and Families. Follow-up data were collected on each case between January 1988 and July 1993 to determine the subjects' recorded involvement in delinquent acts. Since the objective is to establish the causal role of abuse on subsequent delinquency, a matched sample of 220 non-abuse cases in the same agency, in the same period was drawn.

Although the experience of abuse during childhood may increase the probability of delinquent behavior, the path between these two points may not be as simple and direct as we usually assume. The ultimate outcome of the experience of abuse may be influenced by a variety of other factors including the severity of abuse, the gender of the child, the racial group of the child, and the current age of the child. Many other factors may also influence a child's subsequent involvement in delinquent behavior. However, only the severity of abuse, the gender of the child, the racial group of the child, and the current age of the child are addressed in the present research.

This research assesses the effects of childhood abuse on the victim's subsequent involvement in delinquent behavior through research that improves on prior studies in several areas including: (1) the use of a prospective cohort design; (2) incorporation of a control group matched for age, racial group, gender, and SES; (3) clear Operationalization of abuse using only officially reported and validated cases; (4) examination of the first wave of a long-term follow-up; and (5) exploration of the effects of variations in the severity of abuse.

The book is divided in ten chapters. Chapter one introduces and presents a synopsis of the research presented in this book. Chapter two provides a comprehensive review of the existing literature on the consequences of child abuse for an early onset of juvenile delinquency. After a brief introduction, the studies that examine the relationship between abuse and delinquency are discussed. Delinquency is treated as a major outcome of abuse. The studies examining the relationship between child abuse and delinquency have been organized according to the type and form of the methodology utilized. The weaknesses and strengths of the designs utilized by each of these studies are discussed. This is followed by the proposed conceptual framework in chapter three.

Chapter four of the book provides a detailed description of the data, selection of samples, and the methodology. Chapter five presents the hypotheses to be tested in this research and chapter six describes the procedures. Chapter seven presents the analysis. Chapter eight discusses the results. Chapter nine provides summary, conclusions, and suggestions for future research. Chapter ten discusses the policy implications of the results of this study.

Chapter 2

Child Abuse and Delinquency: Empirical View

Since the conceptualization of the "battered child syndrome" (Kempe et al. 1962), child abuse research has "grown geometrically," leading to a major expansion of our knowledge base. Abuse is often hypothesized to have several possible social, social-psychological, and behavioral consequences (Mayall and Norgard, 1983), and a major part of the research on this issue has focused on the adverse consequences of abuse. Some researchers have claimed that early childhood victimization is extremely detrimental to an individual's emotional and social development (Aber et al., 1989; Brown and Finkelhor, 1986; Kinard, 1980; McCormack et al., 1986; Mueller and Silverman, 1991; Friedman and Morse, 1974). Some argue that victims of severe and multiple types of abuse feel less positive about themselves and evince deficits in self-esteem (Oates and Peacock, 1985), self-adjustment (Perry et al., 1983), and more generally in emotional development (Kinard, 1980). Research has documented that child abuse victims are at a considerable risk of problems ranging from minor physical abnormalities such as sleeplessness to poor self-concept (Kinard, 1980), inadequate trust of others (Burgess et al., 1987), weak family ties, developmental deficiencies, runaway risk (Gutierres and Reich, 1981), and acts of serious delinquency such as aggression toward property and persons (Hoffman-Plotkin and Twentyman, 1984).

Many studies have been conducted to examine the relationship between child abuse and subsequent delinquency and crime. The rudimentary hypothesis guiding such research is that delinquency is a direct and inevitable consequence of abuse. Some researchers have postulated that the unlawful and problematic behavior of youths is related to the child's experience of abuse in the early years of life. Most researchers have deemed delinquency and crime as the most significant, probable, and most adverse effects of child abuse because these are the problem behaviors taken to the extreme.

Many of the earlier studies found that a majority of delinquent children had suffered abuse during early years of their lives. Several studies report very high rates of abuse (50% to 75%) among delinquents (Burgess et al., 1987; Lewis et al., 1979; Lynch and Roberts, 1982; Mouzakitis, 1981; Steele and Pollock, 1974).

However, much of this research, due to problems inherent in the methodologies and research designs used, lacks a cautious examination of the association between abuse and delinquency. More methodologically sound studies report that the experience of abuse affects victims but not as devastatingly as some of the earlier studies had suggested (Alfaro, 1981; McCord, 1983; Widom, 1989b; Zingraff et al., 1993).

This chapter assesses empirical evidence from a number of disciplines-- sociology, psychology, psychiatry, medicine, and social work--relating to the consequences of child abuse.

This literature review discusses studies that focus exclusively on the relationship between abuse and delinquency, crime, and problematic behavior. Some of the studies reviewed in this book claim a very direct and significant causal relationship between abuse, delinquency, crime, and problematic behavior. These studies suggest that the cycle of abuse continues through intergenerational transmission whereby victims of abuse often grow up to abuse family as well as other members of society. Other studies reviewed report a more moderate relationship between abuse and delinquency. All of these studies are critically examined from a methodological point of view to explain the disparities in their conclusions. These studies are also critically examined to derive a conceptual framework to explain the relationship between abuse and delinquency and to devise an appropriate methodology to be utilized for a more accurate analysis possible of this relationship.

Research in the area of child abuse and its consequences has been criticized for several design problems that limit the findings' generalizability. One of these problems is weak sampling techniques. Opportunity or convenience samples using data gathered from patients, convicted offenders, medical and psychiatric practitioners, clinical accounts, and small-scale case studies have been the earliest and most common studies. Such samples have limitations because they are not representative of abused or delinquent children. Retrospective data collection, after-the-fact analysis, and the lack of control groups in several of these studies further devalue the usefulness of their findings.

Clinical Studies

These studies are conducted, for the most part, by clinicians using patients, inmates, and other persons who have already manifested some undesirable behavior. Some of these studies report that several of the adolescents who attempted or succeeded in killing their parents had abusive childhoods and that several of the accused or convicted adult murderers have also been the victims of childhood abuse. These studies are discussed below.

Eason and Steinhilber (1961) conducted a study using a clinical sample of eight boys who had committed murders. All eight were from "socially normal," defined as two-parent, middle class, and financially stable, families. However, examination of the childhood histories of t these boys revealed that two of them had a clear history of habitual brutal beatings by parents, and the histories of three others also provided evidence of brutality towards them during their childhood. This study concludes that physical abuse of the subjects during their childhood in the form of brutal beatings had been responsible for murderous attacks by the subjects.

Duncan and Duncan (1971) studied six male prisoners convicted of first-degree murder. They found that the childhood histories of four of these convicted prisoners revealed remorseless brutality at the hands of one or both parents. The other two were psychotic, and no childhood histories could be obtained. Like the Eason and Steinhilber (1961) study cited above, this study concludes that childhood abuse was responsible for the subjects' murderous behavior.

Sendi and Blomgren (1975) conducted a study comparing the histories and behavior of ten adolescents who had committed homicide, ten adolescents who had threatened or attempted murder, and ten other adolescents who were hospitalized for psychiatric problems. These researchers reported that the first two groups were more likely than the third group to have come from home environments where a great amount of abuse and neglect were present.

King (1975) studied nine male adolescents who had committed homicides as teenagers, comparing their childhood histories with those of their siblings. This study found that the adolescents who committed murder were subjected to more severe beatings than their siblings. In another study by Tuteur and Glotzer (1966) ten mothers who had murdered their children were found to have suffered from severe emotional neglect although there was no evidence of abuse.

Ressler and Burgess (1985) conducted a study using a sample (n=31) of sexual murderers who were part of FBI data on sexual homicide and crime scene patterns. They report that 13 of the 31 murderers had been victims of physical abuse, 23 had suffered from psychological abuse, and 12 had been victims of sexual abuse during their childhood.

In another study, Blount and Chandler (1979) reviewed the state hospital records of thirty randomly selected patients between the ages of thirteen and eighteen. Half of these patients (15) had admitted to violent behavior while the other fifteen had no evidence of violent behavior. The hospital records included reports of all previous placements, treatments, and agencies. More of the violent patients (8 out of 15) had an abusive childhood (physical, sexual, or severe deprivation) than did the non-violent patients (3 out of 15).

Climent and Ervin (1972) studied forty violent patients (mean age 28) who were came to Boston City Hospital's emergency room with the chief complaint of violent behavior. These persons reported history of repetitive severe violent acts against persons. These patients and a control group of non-violent patients matched on gender, racial group, religion, and marital status were interviewed in the emergency room. The researchers report that violent patients were more likely to report having experienced physical abuse as children. Physical assaults by fathers were more likely among the violent patients than among the non-violent patients (sixteen out of forty and six out of forty, respectively).

Monane et al. (1984) conducted a study using a sample of 166 children and adolescents between the ages of three and seventeen who were receiving psychiatric services at a large city hospital in 1970. They divided the sample into two groups: those whose medical histories revealed an abusive childhood and those without any history of abuse. Abuse was defined as "deliberate aggressive acts by family members or others outside the family that caused or could have been expected to cause serious injury." Ordinary spankings or beatings on the buttocks with a strap or switch were not considered abuse. The researchers noted that violent behavior was the most significant factor distinguishing the abused from the non-abused psychiatrically hospitalized children and adolescents. They observed that a far higher percentage (72%) of the abused patients had been extremely violent compared with the non-abused patients (46%). They also reported that homicidal behavior was more common among the abused compared with the non-abused group (33% and 24%, respectively).

The results of these studies suggest a simple, straight-forward, and overwhelmingly strong causal relationship between the experience of childhood abuse and subsequent violent behavior.

The major limitation of these studies, however, is that data are collected on patients or convicted inmates who are not representative of all adolescents. This method does not provide an accurate estimate of the probability of delinquency and adult criminal behavior, given child abuse. The conclusion that delinquency and adult criminal behavior are direct consequences given the cause may prove not to be true. It is not surprising that the majority of the subjects in these studies were found to have abusive environments during their childhoods. It is like looking for abnormalities among abnormal people. The very strong observed relationship between abuse, delinquency, and crime in these studies is not generalizable to the total population because it is a consequence of special unrepresentative samples and the use of inappropriate research designs. It may be that the majority of delinquents had an abusive childhood, but we know from several empirical studies that all abused children do not become delinquents. In fact, the majority do not. Other problems that detract from the comparative and predictive significance of the above mentioned studies include the lack of adequate control groups and after-the-fact analysis.

Observational Studies

A number of observational studies have been conducted to examine the relationship between abuse and behavior problems that may precede delinquency. These studies are observational in that they observe abused and control groups in the controlled lab-like environment. These studies focus on the effects of abuse on young children's behavior (e.g., George and Main, 1979; Reidy, 1977; Kinard, 1980).

The review of these studies is important for the fact that if the effects of abuse are evident in these studies (that examine the effects of abuse in very young children and after a short follow-up period), then further examination of the issue among older children is necessary. This review is significant from another perspective as well. Most of these studies examine the effects of abuse on very young children's, including infants' and toddlers' behavior. The results of these studies provide evidence that abused children behave differently when compared with non-abused children. These findings also indicate that the behavior problems observed among young abused children may be predictive of subsequent delinquency and that the effects of abuse become manifest soon after abuse. This implies that it is not absolutely necessary that longer periods have to pass before the effects of abuse can be examined. This insight provides the justification for studying the effects of abuse on the victims after shorter follow-up periods, like the one devised in this study. These studies are discussed below in detail.

Morse et al. (1970) conducted a study using a sample of 25 two-year-Olds who were hospitalized and treated for suspected abuse at Strong Memorial Hospital between 1963 and 1966. These children were followed up approximately three years later. Median age at the time of follow-up was five years. Examination of their histories, including hospital and social services agency records, reveals that six of the 25 children were emotionally disturbed, i.e., were frightened, withdrawn, had temper tantrums, were aggressive and hyperactive, or experienced disciplinary problems. Nine of these 25 children were judged to be mentally retarded as a consequence of abuse. These results indicate that the effects of abuse can be externalizing as well as internalizing. While some of the victims may engage in aggressive behavior and face disciplinary problems, the other victims may feel withdrawn and incapable of taking any initiative on their own as they feel less positive about themselves and their self-concept is badly injured.

Martin and Beezley (1977) identified fifty abused children between the ages of two and ten years and then observed these cases four years after the abuse was first identified. The researchers observed nine characteristics while these children were undergoing physical and neurological examinations, intelligence testing, and interviews. They report that 33 of the fifty had impaired ability for enjoyment, 31 had behavioral symptoms, 26 suffered low self-esteem, twelve suffered from withdrawal, twelve from opposition, eleven from hyper-vigilance, eleven from compulsivity, ten from precocious behavior, and nine experienced school learning problems. Again as in the Morse et al. (1970) study the adverse effects are felt more in the emotional and psychological damage to the victims' self esteem and self concept and less in their involvement in legally problematic behavior.

In 1980, Kinard conducted a study similar to Martin and Beezley (1977) using a sample of thirty abused children and a control group of thirty non-abused children matched for racial group, age, sex, welfare status, birth order, parent structure, and residence. The children were between the ages of five and twelve at the time of study. Children's behavior was rated on the Piers Harris Childhood Self-Concept scale, the Rosenzweig Picture Frustration Study, and the Tasks of Emotional Development, at the time of follow-up. The abused children scored significantly lower on self-concept and socialization than did the non-abused children.

Another study of young children was conducted by Straker and Jacobson (1981) using a sample of nineteen abused children and a control group of nineteen non-abused children aged five to ten years. Physical abuse was verified by the child's admission to the hospital. The researchers utilized a measure of fantasy aggression to assess aggression among abused and non-abused children. They report no differences in aggression among abused and non-abused children. However, the abused children were found to be more emotionally maladjusted and a little less empathetic compared with the non-abused children.

Burgess and Conger (1978) studied a sample of five-to-eight-year-Olds that included seventeen children from abusive families, seventeen children from neglectful families, and seventeen children from control families. The controls were matched on age, income, number of siblings, and education. Compared with controls, the abused children observed in their homes during four separate visits were found to interact less verbally and physically with their mothers. Neglected children spoke less often, interacted less positively, and initiated fewer physical contacts with their fathers. In this study, the controls are adequately matched in order to isolate the effects of abuse from the possible effects of other extraneous factors, and the behaviors are observed directly, although it is unclear how long a follow-up period was allowed for abuse to manifest its effects.

George and Main (1979) studied ten abused toddlers aged one to three and a control group matched for the child's age and racial group, the mother's and father's education and marital status, and the family's living situation. Trained observers noted that compared with the control group, the abused toddlers were more likely to physically assault peers, harass care-givers verbally, assault or threaten to assault care-givers, and avoid other children. Abused children were also less likely to respond to the care-givers' response to friendly gestures.

Wassermann and Allen (1983) compared twelve physically abused fourteen-month-old infants to the non-abused infants matched on age, sex, racial group, and SES. Mother-infant interactions were videotaped during free play situations. The infants were measured on cognitive and social competence. Compared with controls, the abused infants were more likely to ignore or refuse maternal distractions but equally likely to comply with orders from the mother. This significant finding suggests that the infants may already have learned to comply with the mother's order in an effort to escape physical abuse.

Bousha and Twentyman (1984) compared abused, neglected, and control group children's behavior through naturalistic observations in the child's home for ninety minutes on each of three consecutive days. Their sample included twelve abused child-mother pairs, twelve neglected child-mother pairs, and twelve control child-mother pairs. All of the children were four years old. These children were rated on their interactions with their mothers. The abused and neglected children showed fewer positive verbal and non-verbal behaviors while they displayed more aggressive behavior than control group children. The neglected children manifested more verbal and nonverbal aggression and had fewer interactions with their mothers compared with both abused and control children.

Reidy (1977) conducted a study of twenty abused, sixteen neglected, and 22 control six and seven-year-old children. Teachers observed and rated these children on a behavior problems checklist during fantasy and free play. Abused children were found to be more aggressive than the neglected children or the controls. Hoffman-Plotkin and Twentyman (1984) reported heightened aggression among the abused children compared with the non-abused children. These researchers observed behavior of fourteen abused, fourteen neglected, and fourteen control group children aged 49 to 51 months. Children's behavior was observed in the classroom for thirty minutes and was rated by both parents and teachers. Abused and neglected children scored significantly higher on aggressiveness and anti-social behavior and significantly lower on social maturity and readiness to learn compared with the control group children. However, the researchers report no difference on measures of social interaction with teachers, noncompliance, disruptive behavior, or affection to others.

A similar study was conducted by Perry et al. (1983) comparing the behavior of 21 abused children with 21 non-abused children four to six years old. Children were assessed on the Washington Symptom Checklist (63 types of behavior) by their mothers. The mothers of abused children were more likely to assess their children to have abnormal behavior, poor self concept, and lower school adjustment than were the mothers of non-abused children. In another study, Aragona and Eyberg (1981) examined 27 mother-child dyads selected from clinical and research files for the years of 1976-1978. These dyads were divided into three categories: neglected children, abused children with behavior problems, and children with no problems. All of these children were white and between the ages of five and six. Children's behavior problems were measured on the Eyberg Child Behavior Inventory by information provided by the mothers. Children with behavior problems scored higher on the Inventory compared with neglected and control group children.

Wolfe (1985) examined behavior problems and social competence by sampling 102 children from violent families and 96 children from nonviolent families in Ontario. These children were between the ages of four and sixteen. The mothers were asked to rate their children's behavior on the Achenbach Child Behavior Checklist, which provides ratings of a child's social competence (for example, hyperactivity, aggression, and withdrawal) and to provide information on maternal stress and family violence. Children from the violent families were rated significantly higher on behavior problems and lower on social competence as compared with the children from the nonviolent families. A far higher proportion of the children from the violent families (34% of the boys and 20% of the girls) fell within the clinical range of behavior problems compared with the children from the nonviolent families (15% of the boys and 5% of the girls).

Jaffee et al. (1986) studied the effects of direct and indirect violence on school age boys by comparing a sample of 32 boys from shelters for battered women who had witnessed violence among their parents with a sample of eighteen boys from a provincial child-welfare agency who had been physically abused by their parents. They established a control group by placing a newspaper advertisement asking women and children to participate in a study of family relations. Children in this study were matched on age and SES. The mothers were asked to rate their children's behavior on the Achenbach Child Behavior Checklist. Significant differences were found in the behavior of the three groups' behavior. Both the abused and the exposed-to-violence groups differed from the control group on externalizing and internalizing scores, and the abused boys showed more externalizing symptoms as compared with the exposed-to-violence children. The boys who were exposed to family violence had adjustment problems similar to those of the abused children but different from those exhibited by the control group children.

Other studies involving young children have reported no differences in behavior between abused and non-abused children. For example, Friedreich et al. (1983) compared abilities and behavior of eleven physically abused preschool male children with those of ten non-abused children. The controls were matched for child's age, family income, and mother's education and age. The children were measured on the McCarthy Scales of children's abilities, the Wide Range Achievement Test, and the Child's Performance on a Persistence Task. The researchers report significant differences between abused and non-abused subjects' cognitive development, verbal abilities, and memory (abused children scored significantly lower than non-abused children) but report no behavioral differences between the two groups. These findings directly contradict the findings reported in the other studies reviewed above but alert us to the significant effects that abuse may have on its victims. The experience of abuse may cause internalizing as well as externalizing disorders and these effects are not mutually exclusive.

These observational studies are more sophisticated in method and research design. Almost all have control groups that are generally well matched with the abused children on racial group, age, gender, SES, and other relevant parental background characteristics. Abuse is carefully defined. All of the researchers used substantiated cases and collected data prospectively. Consequently, the results of the observational studies are more reliable than the results of the clinical studies. However, the findings of some of the studies (Reidy, 1977; Hoffman-Plotkin and Twentyman, 1984; Perry et al., 1983; Aragona and Eyberg, 1981) are questionable because of the fact that assessments of the child's behavior were made on the basis of information provided by parents or teachers whose judgment may have been influenced by the prior knowledge of the children's abuse as well as their own personal attitudes toward the children.   Such subjective evaluations are even more problematical when the informants were abusers as was the case in the study by Perry et al. (1983), Wolfe, (1985) and Jaffee (1986).

Despite the differences in methodologies used to measure outcomes, reports of some of these observational studies indicate with some consistency, that abuse has a significant effect on the victims. The effects could be realized by internalizing or externalizing disorders, or both, under different circumstances. Some studies claim that the abused children exhibited heightened problematic behavior even at early ages. For example, the abused infants ignored or refused maternal distractions (Wassermann and Allen, 1983); the abused toddlers assaulted their peers and harassed care-givers (George and Main, 1979); the abused children were more aggressive in fantasy and free play (Reidy, 1977); and the abused children were emotionally maladjusted, particularly in the development of self concept (Kinard, 1980). Other studies (Wassermann and Allen, 1983; Friedreich et al., 1983; and Straker and Jacobson, 1981) show that there were not any significant differences among the abused and the non-abused children's behavior.

The results of the observational studies provide a basis for the concept that abuse's sequelae are multidimensional and the victims get affected in several different ways. In some of these studies, the adverse effects of abuse were evident at a very early age, which indicates that abuse does not, necessarily, need longer follow-up periods to manifest its effects. As is evident from the results of several studies reviewed above, abused children have more behavior problems as compared with non-abused children. These behavior problems may be the foundation of delinquency observed in older children.

These results also suggest that abuse has adverse effect on the victims' self esteem and may thwart their capabilities for self initiative. This may explain the lower problematic behaviors discerned by some of the studies or no difference in the behavior between the abused and the non-abused subjects. This alerts us to the magnitude of the damage abuse may be able to cause to the victim. The results also suggest that an abusive environment is conducive to learning and internalizing the abusive mode of interactions.

Survey Design Studies

Another large group of studies that suggests a strong association between abuse and delinquency employs survey methodology. Some important examples from this group are discussed below.

Kratcoski (1985) administered questionnaires to youths referred to a juvenile justice center because of their delinquent behavior and to a control group of high school students. The self-report questionnaires asked for demographics and the information on each youth's family functioning, parental attitude towards youth (particularly aggressive behavior towards youth), peer group relations, school functioning and violence committed while in peer group settings. The questionnaires also asked for the type and frequency of violent acts committed by the subjects in both groups. Kratcoski reports that youths who were violent towards their parents and had expressed violence towards their siblings, had experienced violence from their parents and had observed parents reacting to each other in a violent manner to a much higher degree than those who were not violent towards their parents and siblings. He comments that in some cases a youth's act of violence towards a parent was a reaction to the parent's act of violence towards the youth or an action to protect the other parent or sibling who was being beaten by a spouse, boyfriend or another person in the household. He adds that in several cases the youth's violence toward the parent was a reaction to the parent's effort to assert authority over the youth. This very significant finding suggests that abuse not only makes victims angry but also incites them to imitate this mode of behavior.

Mouzakitis (1981) administered questionnaires to a group of sixty adjudicated teenage female delinquents in the Arkansas Girls Training School. Overall, 86% of the respondents in this study reported that they had received physical punishment by the use of hands, objects, or belts. Out of these, 51% recalled bruises, 25% recalled scars, and 38% recalled having bled from the beatings. About 20% did not remember any physical effects. Seventy-two percent of those who recalled receiving physical punishment as children described receiving this punishment before the age of ten. In all, 25% reported that they had been physically abused since infancy. It seems that physical punishment was not a response to the incorrigibility or delinquency of these girls since most of them reported having experienced abuse before the age of ten.

Hartstone and Hansen (1984) conducted a study of 114 juvenile male offenders who had been found guilty of excessively violent offenses against persons and who had prior adjudications for felonious crimes against persons or property. The data were gathered from official records in the case files of the subjects, structured interviews with the subjects, and retrospective accounts from the subjects' mother or mother figures. The results of this study show that 30% of the group had witnessed or experienced at least one form of family violence directed towards them or another member of their family; 23% had evidence in the case file or stated that their fathers had engaged in beating their mothers; 15% had suffered from prior child abuse (defined as physical violence); and 2% had been sexually abused. The researchers caution that since family violence is under reported in both client and case files, the results of their study may be an underestimate of the actual abuse among these juveniles.

Geller and Ford-Somma (1984) conducted a study of the effects of abuse on violent delinquency by studying a group of 226 incarcerated juvenile offenders in a training school in New Jersey. This study is worth considering in some detail because of some far reaching implications. These researchers administered self-report questionnaires to the whole group and then conducted interviews with a sub-sample of 22 offenders. A majority of the offenders reported having experienced some form of family violence. Overall 66% reported having been beaten with a belt or extension cord, 32% reported having been beaten repeatedly, 20% reported that they had been threatened with a knife or a gun. A total of 33% reported having been beaten so harshly that they were bruised; 29% bled; and 8% required hospitalization. These juveniles reported not only having experienced violence but also having perpetrated violence. Twenty-two percent reported punching their fathers; 5% reported attacking fathers with a knife or gun; 12% reported hitting siblings with a stick or other hard object; and 9% had beaten their siblings so hard that they bled.

Geller and Ford-Somma (1984) conducted regression analyses to determine the relationship between experiencing violence and perpetrating violence. Violent delinquency (the dependent variable) was measured by the number of times an offender was arrested for murder, armed robbery, robbery without the use of weapon, rape, assault with weapon, or "beating someone for the hell of it." Forms of family violence (the independent variables) were divided into three categories: routine family violence, life-threatening violence, and injurious violence. Routine family violence was measured by the number of times an offender had been hit with a belt, stick, or some other hard object. Life-threatening violence was measured by the number of times the offender was threatened or assaulted with a knife or gun. Injurious violence was measured by the number of times offenders were beaten so badly that they bruised or bled (Geller and Ford-Somma, 1984: 54-55).

The key finding of this research was that the more offenders had been victimized by routine violence, the more violent crimes they committed. The most common form of family violence--routine family violence--had the most significant effect on the victim who later became a perpetrator of violence in and outside the home. Life-threatening and injurious family violence did not appear to have a significant impact on violent delinquency. This is a significant finding. The fact that injurious and life threatening family violence, though severe, did not turn the victims as violent as routine family violence did, indicates that extreme severe and multiple types of abuse may damage the victim's emotions and emotional development to an extent that the victim loses any desire, motivation, and ability to take an initiative.

Geller and Ford-Somma (1984) performed another analysis using expressive violent crimes (defined by them as murder, rape, assault with a weapon, and "beating for the hell of it") as the dependent variable. This analysis explained 14% of the variance with both routine and life-threatening family violence contributing significantly. In another regression, these researchers found that none of the independent variables was significantly related to instrumental violence (robbery and armed robbery).

Hotalling et al. (1989) analyzed survey data from general population samples to assess the effects of family violence. Data on child abuse were derived from parent self reports. Parents were asked to report if they "kicked, bit, or hit with a knife or gun" any of their children within the past year. These researchers also generated self report measures of spouse assault, sibling assault, and assault of non-family members. They report that one in every six children in the United States had been severely assaulted by parents during the year that the survey was conducted. In addition, they also report that the children abused by their parents had higher rates of assault against siblings, parents, and persons outside the family compared with the non-abused children. Rates become higher among children who were both assaulted and witnessed assaults on other family members.

These studies (Geller and Ford-Somma, 1984; Hotalling et al., 1989) suggest a conceptual framework for interpreting the association between abuse and delinquency: An individual who is subjected to violence routinely in the family learns and models that behavior. As Straus et el. (1980) comment, "Each generation learns to be violent by being a participant in a violent family." The abusive environment in the family provides not only experience to internalize but also helps the individual by providing the models. Families where violence is the norm, serve as training grounds for the children who learn and adopt that mode of interaction as their own.

Longitudinal Retrospective Studies

Retrospective studies have also been used to examine the relationship between child abuse and subsequent delinquency. This section includes two types of retrospective studies: (1) Retrospective studies with control groups (for example Glueck and Glueck, 1950 and Lewis and Shanok, 1977); (2) Retrospective studies without control groups (for example Wick, 1981; and Kratcoski, 1982). The first set of studies are case control studies and are often used in epidemiology and medicine and these studies include control groups.

Although these studies have contributed a great deal to this area of research, the design has its own limitations. Most of these studies claim a strong relationship between abuse and delinquency. However, this strong association could be the consequence of the after-the-fact analyses of preexisting records. Most of the survey design studies examine the association between abuse and delinquency by studying only those subjects who have become delinquent rather than a representative sample of all abused children. This may not precisely estimate the probability of delinquency, given abuse. Here, we will look briefly at a few representative retrospective studies.

The most often cited retrospective study was conducted by Glueck and Glueck (1950). They compared 500 institutionalized delinquents with 500 non-delinquents, matching the two samples for age, racial group, IQ, and neighborhood of origin to determine if their families had been reported for abuse or neglect of their children and were thus in need of assistance from social services agencies. They found that 85% of the families of the delinquents were classified as abusive or neglectful compared with 44% of the families of non-delinquents.

Lewis and Shanok (1977) compared 109 adjudicated delinquents with a control group of 109 non-delinquents matched for age, racial group, gender, and SES. Hospital records revealed that 9% of delinquent youths had been treated for injuries secondary to abuse compared with 1% of the non-delinquents. In a subsequent analysis, Lewis et al. (1979) studied 97 boys incarcerated at a correctional center in Connecticut. A child psychiatrist and a neurologist evaluated each child on a violence scale from one (least violent) to four (most violent) based on the evidence of his having committed any offense against a person or property. The evaluators also attempted to obtain as detailed a medical history as possible to determine whether the child had been the victim of abuse. The delinquents who manifested more violent behavior were more likely to have experienced abuse or to have witnessed extreme violence during their childhood than were the non-violent delinquents.

Wick (1981) examined fifty randomly selected case files from 3027 cases of "youth in trouble" referred to the Central Texas Youth Service Bureau because of the behavior that was considered unacceptable by the community, including problematic nondelinquent acts as well as legally defined delinquent acts (p. 234). These children ranged between the ages of five and eighteen. The case files were analyzed to determine the severity and the source of each child's problems. In 29% of the cases, the youths' troubles were determined to result primarily from abuse or neglect. Surveying 863 case files of delinquent male adolescents who were incarcerated for serious offenses in four Ohio institutions, Kratcoski (1982) found that 26% (223 out of 863) of the delinquent cases had experienced physical abuse in some form during their childhood. Kratcoski's study design is superior to most other retrospective studies because he used a clear definition of child abuse and used only validated cases of physical abuse.

Even though the methodology of retrospective studies has limitations, it is significant that virtually all such studies consistently show a strong relationship between abuse and delinquency. This indicates that some relationship between these two phenomena may be existing although this relationship may not be of such magnitude as these retrospective studies assert. This points to the need for the development of better research designs to study the consequences of abuse.

Longitudinal Prospective Studies

Studies using a longitudinal prospective design are more sophisticated than the other study designs discussed above. Unlike the after-the-fact analysis of retrospective studies, prospective studies begin with the event (abuse in this case) and follow the individual until adolescence or adulthood in order to examine the effects of the event that took place in childhood. Some prospective studies (Widom, 1989a; Widom, 1989b) use adequately matched control groups to eliminate alternative hypotheses and extraneous variables, and most also use substantiated official records, which further enhance the validity of their findings by eliminating problems of recall and social desirability bias. The use of large samples and long follow-up periods between the two events (30 years in Widom's 1989c study; 40 years in McCord's 1983 and 1986 studies) make the findings more reliable. Consequently, the results of the studies utilizing longitudinal prospective designs present a more reasonable picture of the association between abuse and delinquency.

Widom (1989c) used a longitudinal prospective design. Beginning with the hypothesized cause (abuse), she identified a sample of 908 abused and neglected children from the 1967 to 1971 records of a midwestern court and selected a control group (n=667) matched for age, racial group, gender, and SES. She then established base rates of delinquency and crime for the control group through a search of the subject's local, state, and federal criminal records covering a period of twenty to thirty years. These base rates were compared with the delinquency and crime rates among the abused group. Widom's findings indicate that the majority of abused children (71.4%) did not have delinquent or criminal records. However, the abused subjects were slightly more likely to have delinquent and criminal records than were the matched control group subjects (28.6% versus 21.1%).

The several strengths of this study include its prospective design, its adequately matched control group, its use of substantiated abuse cases, and its large sample size. The design and conceptualization of Widom's study represent a substantial improvement over previous research.

Using case records, McCord (1983) identified 232 subjects who were originally reported for abuse and neglect between 1939 and 1945. These subjects were retraced and followed up between 1975 and 1979, providing a forty-year perspective on the consequences of child abuse. The subjects were divided into four subgroups--those who were abused, neglected, loved, or rejected by their parents during childhood. Men who had been subjected to consistently punitive physical punishments were classified as abused. Men whose parents showed neither affection nor rejection and had very few interactions with their children were classified as neglected. Men who had at least one parent who seemed concerned about the child's welfare and pleased with the child's behavior were classified as loved. Men whose parents neither abused, neglected, nor cared for the children were classified as rejected. Serious crimes were committed in adulthood by 50% of the rejected children, 20% of the abused children, and about 11% of the loved children.

The strength of this study lies in its design. It was prospective, had a control group, and was based on the observations of behavior of the boys in their homes. However, the Operationalization of measures for group assignment and the labeling of the children as abused, neglected, loved, or rejected leaves a sense of uneasiness about the validity of the assessment. Nevertheless, the study is significant because it was the first one to examine the continuation of the effects of abuse into adulthood.

Another well-known prospective longitudinal study by McCord (1986) reports similar findings. She identified 253 inner city boys who were visited twice a month during 1939 to 1945 as part of the Cambridge Somerville Youth Project's delinquency prevention program. These boys and their family members were rated on a number of dimensions based on the notes of the social workers who observed the interactions between these boys and their parents over a six-year period. Long term follow-up (thirty to forty years) of these subjects during 1975 to 1979 indicated that at least 33% of the subjects had been convicted of serious crimes.

McCord (1986) constructed dichotomous scales and unidimensional clusters to identify criminogenic families. The boys who became criminals had parents who were harshly punitive and lacked affection in the treatment of their sons. Marital conflict, inconsistent discipline, parental deviance, lack of supervision, and low expectations for the child were additional criminogenic conditions. This study reports that paternal aggressiveness and maternal permissiveness were the most critical exacerbating factors contributing to criminality and that maternal affection, maternal self confidence, and paternal respect for the mother were the insulating factors against criminality.

Despite the fact that this study is a prospective longitudinal one, it has some limitations. The operational definitions used to classify parents are vague, and the criteria for identifying abuse do not correspond clearly to the typical definitions of abuse. Harsh punitive treatment, aggression, and the lack of affection are equated with abuse. For example, parents who "yelled, threw things, or attempted to injure someone when frustrated or angry" were classified as aggressive and therefore abusive, even though this kind of aggressiveness is not necessarily the same as abuse. However, the study is important because of the long period for the manifestation of the consequences of abuse. The study also points to some of the mediating factors, e.g., maternal affection, maternal self-confidence, and paternal respect for mothers, that tend to insulate victims from the negative effects of abuse and help them remain resilient in the face of adversity.

Alfaro (1981) conducted a prospective study involving 4465 children who had been referred to protection agencies for suspected abuse or neglect in 8 New York State counties from 1952 to 1953. During the following fifteen years, 17.2% of these subjects had at least one contact with the juvenile court for delinquency or ungovernability. Bolton et al. (1977) report the results of another prospective study of a sample of 5392 children who had been referred to the Arizona State Department of

Economic Security for sexual, physical, or emotional abuse. Of this group, 873 were subsequently identified as appearing in juvenile court records as dependency and delinquency cases, although the time period over which this study was conducted is not specified. Ninety-nine were dependency cases, and 774 (14.3% of the original sample of 5392) were referred for delinquent behavior. The lack of a control group in the studies by Alfaro (1981) and Bolton et al. (1977) reduces the usefulness of their findings because no comparisons can be made on the basis of their findings and it is difficult to examine the exclusive effects of abuse.

Zingraff et al. (1993) used a prospective research design to examine delinquency among abused children and compare it with non-abused school and non-abused poor children. They found that while the abused children had a higher delinquency rate than the non-abused children, the differences were not of such a magnitude as the earlier studies had claimed.

These prospective studies (McCord, 1983, McCord, 1986, Widom, 1989c, and Zingraff et al. 1993) will be discussed in further detail later in comparison with the results of this study.

The literature review presented in the earlier section of this chapter demonstrates the state of the research in child abuse and delinquency area. Despite a tendency among many researchers to assume a simple direct connection between abuse and delinquency, my understanding of the literature leads me to believe that the relationship between abuse and delinquency is much more complex.

However, the findings of the studies in this literature review indicate that abuse can affect its victims' perceptions, attitudes, behavior, and eventually their actions. Delinquency may not result so much from abuse as from the chain of events that follow abuse. It is likely that the interim effects of abuse have a significant impact on the eventual outcome, making delinquency and crime the indirect consequences of abuse rather than the direct outcomes. For example, severe forms of physical abuse may cause developmental deficits which in turn affect the child's capabilities and perceptions. These deficits may lead to poor self-concept, a need to associate with other children like oneself, a lack of belief in good behavior, a lack of attachment, and a whole host of other problems that may influence the child to become involved in delinquency. Abuse may lead to changed environments or family conditions that may in turn affect the child's subsequent behavior and involvement in delinquency. A child running away from an abusive person may become vulnerable to many incidents that may eventually lead to delinquent behavior. Or, a child who is routinely subjected to physical beatings may become desensitized to pain and less responsive to not only to his or her own pain but also less emotionally responsive to others' feelings, which in turn may influence his or her subsequent behavior. On the other hand, the experience of severe abuse may impede the child's motivation, capabilities, desire, and self-initiative powers. Whether or not abuse eventually leads to delinquent behavior may depend on other events that occur in the child's life. Much existing research suggests that poor self-esteem, lack of self-confidence, withdrawal, and inability to take any initiative are the most serious and less studied effects of the experience of abuse.

Chapter 3

An Integrated Framework: Social Learning and Social Control Theories: Explaining Abuse and Delinquency

Although most of the existing research is atheoretical and this research is unable to test the theoretical concepts as well, the literature provides empirical data and potential for the development of an integrated conceptual framework explaining the association between abuse and delinquency.

Several recent studies have suggested an association between child abuse and subsequent delinquency. The mechanisms by which the abuse of children transforms them into delinquents have not been fully explored. In other words, there is no theoretical framework to explain this association and this presents a special challenge to the researcher. Although this research does not test the conceptual framework presented here, it will be used to form hypotheses to be tested in this study, and to interpret the existing literature and the results of this study.

Child abuse may be regarded as a complex experience consisting of several interrelated components rather than a single phenomenon. To comprehend the connection between child abuse and delinquency, the whole phenomenon needs to be understood. We need to understand the processes and dynamics of the abuse that encourage or discourage involvement in delinquency. We need to understand what it is about abuse that increases the abused children's chances of engaging in delinquency. Is it a desire for retribution, is it an experience that has been internalized and adapted as behavior, or is it that abuse weakens their bonds to adults and society and makes them vulnerable to engage in delinquent behavior if the right opportunities arise?

We need to understand the context and circumstances in which abuse occurs and examine how these serve as triggers or buffers for delinquency.

In most cases, child abuse occurs within the intimate environment of the home and the abuser is often an adult care-taker. The traumatic experience of abuse is not an isolated event but more often than not it is a part of harsh and punitive child-rearing, a home environment that conveys hostility and rejection and perhaps even a blaming of the child for the abuse as well as for every other problem in the adult's life.

Family disorganization as a consequence of stress, marital strife, poverty, unemployment, drug and alcohol addiction may further exacerbate the subsequent adverse effects of child abuse on the victim. Each of these components of child abuse contributes to the development of an environment conducive to antisocial and delinquent behavior (McCord, 1983).

The relationship between child abuse and delinquency seems quite logical. It makes sense that an individual who has been abused as a child would want to retaliate against society whenever he or she can. Delinquent behavior can be seen as an action against society, avenging the abuse that the individual went through as a confused and terrified child.

This section discusses two theoretical frameworks, developed by criminologists to explain delinquency, that have the potential to be utilized to explain the connection between child abuse and juvenile delinquency. With this discussion a conceptual framework that might represent the beginning of a theoretical statement on the relationship is presented.

The purpose of a conceptual framework is to identify explicitly concepts, assumptions, and other information pertinent to the research and lay the groundwork for interpreting existing literature and building a systematic, cohesive theory (Merton, 1968). Inasmuch as a framework is designed to provide a general orientation to the topic it is a "conceptual map" that orients a reader to the terms and relationships that structure the research agenda.

Researchers in the area of child abuse and its consequences for delinquency have not been particularly adept at providing conceptual frameworks for their endeavors. With some notable exceptions (Aber and Allen, 1987; Aber et al., 1989; Egeland and Sroufe, 1981b; George and Main, 1979; Klimes-Dougan and Kistner, 1990; Newberger et al. 1983; Patterson, 1976, 1979), a majority of the research examining an association between child abuse and juvenile delinquency or other aberrant behavior has generally been atheoretical.

There is very little theoretical research done on the subject by sociologists or criminologists. Despite the lack of any theory applied in the existing research, a sociological conceptual framework borrowing some concepts of social learning theory (Patterson et al. 1975; Bandura, 1977;

Akers, 1985; and Patterson, 1982) and social control theory (Hirschi, 1969) can be applied to explain the sequelae of abuse and to inform our understanding of the connection between child abuse and delinquency. While this research does not claim to be testing a conceptual framework, due to the limitations of data, it is an attempt to develop a conceptual framework inferred from the empirical findings and concepts from the existing theories of delinquency.

Social Learning Theory

Social learning theory posits that behavior is controlled by environmental shaping and indirect environmental and developmental influences which include interactions with parents, peers, social institutions (such as schools, churches etc.). Behavior is maintained by the effects it has on the environment. As situations change, behavior will change to fit the new circumstances. People use models for information about what actions are appropriate to particular situations. An observer perceives which responses produce valued ends or avoid unpleasant consequences for a model. Both social and nonsocial situations are discriminative for learning and reinforcement of delinquent behavior.

Two concepts of the social learning theory, **modeling** and **reinforcement**, appear to be particularly useful to think through some of the effects that the independent and the intervening variables are hypothesized to have on delinquency.

It has been demonstrated empirically that children tend to imitate and model the behavior of adults with whom they identify most strongly. Parents, other adult care-takers, and teachers are most certainly the closest adults with whom children are associated.

> These groups influence people by providing *models for imitation*, or modeling the behavior of others. Imitation is engaging in behavior after observation of similar behavior. . . . Whether models' behavior will be imitated is affected by several factors, including characteristics of the models and the observed behavior (Akers, 1985, pp. 46).

If children are raised in an environment where they are abused and where abuse is the principal method used by adults to control the children's behavior, then the children are likely to grow up feeling that this is an appropriate way to deal with children and people who have less power and status and, perhaps, to deal with all kinds of problems, conflicts, and stresses. Consequently children raised in families where abuse is the mode of interpersonal interaction are socialized in that particular manner and are likely to grow up to be like the adults who raised them. This phenomenon has led scholars and others to assert that "abused children will grow up to be abusers," or "violence begets violence" (Curtis, 1963). These assertions have yet to be confirmed as empirical findings, but have led some researchers to assume a simple and direct relationship between being abused and becoming abusive (Spinetta and Rigler, 1972; Gelles, 1980; Gil, 1973; Neapolitan-Jerry, 1981). We know from the literature that not all abused children grow up to be abusers, most do not model their behavior after the abusive parent or caretaker. This is where the second concept, **reinforcement,** helps to explain the phenomenon.

Early exposure to a harsh and punitive parental figure and repeated abuse from such a close adult may have several adverse effects. Imitation and modeling of the abusive behavior may facilitate identification with the abuser. The children may start believing that the observed abusive mode of interaction is an appropriate, and in fact the only appropriate mode of interaction. Eventually the children may internalize that mode of interaction. In some cases the abuser may blame the abused child for all the abuser's own problems, stresses, and other related inadequacies. The abused child may remind the abuser of his or her own weaknesses, unacceptable idiosyncrasies, and impulses. The child becomes a source of relief for the abuser who relieves his or her tensions by abusing the child. The child, unaware of the illogical nature of this process, assumes that he or she is worthy of blame and abuse; this may in turn increase his or her self-hatred and lower self-esteem and may eventually lead to delinquent, especially self-destructive, behavior.

Reinforcement can be used to explain why only a few rather than all abused children grow up to manifest abusive, antisocial, and/or delinquent behavior. Even when individuals have witnessed or experienced a particular behavior, controlled experimentation with modeling shows that if there is no social reinforcement, the behavior will usually be extinguished. This observational learning is more complicated (Akers, 1985) than immediate and direct imitation. That is, individuals do not immediately and directly learn every action they experience or observe. The learning and reinforcement process is subject to   several characteristics of the individuals (such as gender, age, and race) and social environment (such as intensity of the experience, duration of the experience, magnitude of the consequences etc.). Baldwin and Baldwin (1981) emphasize the role of reinforcement further,

> Observers tend to imitate modeled behavior if they like or respect the model, see the model receive reinforcement, see the model give off signs of pleasure, or are in an environment where imitating the model's performance is

reinforced. There are times when an observer does the opposite from the model. This inverse imitation is common when an observer does not like the model, sees the model get punished, or is in an environment where conformity is punished (Baldwin and Baldwin, 1981).

Based on this concept from the social learning perspective, it is hypothesized[1] that abuse may affect children and reinforce abusive behavior in two very opposite ways. (1) If the child who has experienced abuse continues to live in an environment where that sort of behavior is tolerated, condoned, and reinforced, he or she is more likely to internalize that mode of interaction. (2) It may also work to reinforce "inverse imitation". If the abused child does not like the abuser, realizes the extent of pain such an abusive behavior causes, he or she may detest engaging in any behavior that will cause pain to others, etc.

Thus, abuse may increase the victims' chances of engaging in delinquency if they felt that the abuse was legitimate, rewarded, and tolerated; and decrease their chances of engaging in delinquency if they felt that the abuse was bad, painful, undesirable, and the abuser was a detested individual.

Social Control Theory

The second perspective that can be used to explain the abuse delinquency relationship is social control. Social control theory posits that delinquency takes place when an individual's bonds to society are broken or weakened. Individuals conform to the norms and laws because they fear violations will rupture their relationships with family, friends, neighbors, jobs, and school etc. In other words individuals maintain conformity because they do not want their personal image held by important groups (of which they are members) to be tarnished. These bonds to society consist of four components: attachment, commitment, involvement, and belief (Hirschi, 1969).

Attachment refers to the bonds to others such as family, peers, and important institutions such as schools or churches. Weak or no attachment to parents may impair personality development and enhance chances of being involved in delinquent acts. Commitment involves the degree to which an individual maintains a vested interest in the social and economic system. Involvement entails engagement in legitimate social and recreational activities which either leaves too little time to get into trouble or binds one's status to yet other important groups whose opinion one does not wish to blemish. Finally, belief in the conventional norms and value system and the law acts as a bond to society.

According to the social control perspective, weakened or severed bonds increase the likelihood of juveniles engaging in delinquency since they have no personal stakes in conformity. These weakened bonds are the consequence of weakened attachment, commitment, involvement, and belief. Abused children are very likely to have weakened bonds because their environment is not nurturing and fails to provide them with opportunities to develop strong bonds. The significant adults in their lives are the ones who abuse them. Consequently, they may fail to develop attachment with an individual who abused them; to have any commitment to the social or economic system that failed in protecting them; have any belief or faith in adults or society since nobody came to their rescue; and finally perhaps have no involvement in legitimate recreational activities. From this perspective, it can be inferred that abuse provides a very conducive environment for the victim to get involved in delinquency.

Based on the concepts borrowed from the social learning and social control perspectives, it can be deduced that abuse and an abusive environment provide excellent conditions to increase the likelihood of the victim to be involved in delinquency. Reinforcement of the nonconforming behavior is more probable among children who have learnt nonconforming behavior through the experience of abuse and have developed weak or no bonds due to abuse and an abusive environment.

The abused child may develop actual physical and psychological defects which will reinforce the blame. The child may begin to accept the blame for the abuse because it may be the easiest way for the child to survive in the given environment. The parents may reinforce the child's feelings of guilt by ignoring the child when he or she is not disruptive causing the child to further internalize the negative self-image that may serve as the prototype for subsequent anti-social or delinquent behavior. The child may grow up with that negative self image and become involved in cruel and sadistic relationships similar to the one he or she as a child had with adults. Or he or she may reject the negative self-image by means of projection and externalization onto others.

As we see, then, from the social learning perspective, abusive interactions among family members provide a likely model for the acceptance of learning delinquent behavior and for the appropriateness of such behavior (Bandura, 1973) and from the social control perspective, abusive interactions may result in weak or broken bonds. Thus, children learn behavior, at least in part, by imitating and modeling someone else's behavior and when such behavior is reinforced through rewards and punishments, and they are more likely to engage in such behavior if they have no personal stakes in conformity. Straus et al. (1980) commented,

"Each generation learns to be violent by being a participant in a violent family." Although this research will not test the concepts of the framework presented here because of the limited data available on the subjects, this framework will be utilized to guide formulation of our hypotheses and interpret results. This framework is also suggested for future research examining the relationship between abuse and delinquency.

Based on this conceptual model and recognizing the limitations of the data used for this study, it is assumed that the experience and observation of abuse socialize victims to an abusive environment and mode of interaction and reinforce the attitude that the norm for adults is to be harsh, authoritative, and punitive toward children (Rosenberg, 1987; Hershorn and Rosenbaum, 1985; Hughes et al., 1989). Such socialization may weaken their bonds to the society and encourage children who have begun to display behavioral and interpersonal dysfunctions to misbehave more and grow up to be like the adult models in their lives.

The children's belief that nobody cares for their feelings and that the best way, or perhaps the only way, to get people to behave is through harsh, punitive means may encourage their further involvement in delinquency. The experience of abuse may also reinforce the behavior by making the child see and realize the consequences of abuse as providing relief and sometimes even pleasure to the abuser. Thus, abused children are likely to be different from the non-abused who have not been exposed to abuse through experience or observation in certain ways. They are likely to develop either externalizing or internalizing deficits. The children who develop externalizing deficits may engage more in delinquent behavior as compared with the non-abused children. On the other hand, children who develop internalizing deficits may become withdrawn and lack most of the social skills to an extent that they are less likely to engage in any kind of social interaction that requires initiative and taking risk. Thus, such children will have lower delinquency than the non-abused children. Consequently, it is hypothesized that abused children will differ from non-abused children and the difference could go either way.

Socialization experiences differ by gender and by racial group. Different social conditions determine the differential modeling, reinforcement, and development of bonds. Males are socialized to be aggressive, independent, and stand up for themselves. Consequently, the experience of abuse is expected to affect them differently as compared with females who are socialized to be dependent, submissive, patient, forgiving, and tolerant. The experience of abuse may incite the learning instincts of males to stand up and fight for their rights and they may model the abusive behavior and learn more easily and eagerly to engage in delinquent behavior as compared to females. Females, due to their socialization norms and expectations, may accept the abuse as a normal part of life, forgive the abuser and turn this into a experience teaching and reinforcing withdrawal, lower self-concept, and self-blame etc.

It is hypothesized that females will engage less in an externalizing behavior, such as delinquency, as compared with males even though they might have experienced similar kinds of abuse. The reason for this hypothesis is that our gendered socialization norms expect females to be tolerant, passive, and submissive while males are expected to be aggressive, active, and fight for their rights. These socialization norms lead us to hypothesize that females will suffer more from internalizing than externalizing deficits (which this research can not examine). Consequently the difference in delinquency referrals will be bigger between abused and non-abused for males than for females. These socialized norms may also increase the probability for males to sever their bonds with society more easily as compared with females who by nature and socialization are more tolerant, patient, and forgiving. The females may not develop as weak bonds as males despite the similar experience of abuse. Thus, it is likely that females will have lower rate of delinquency referrals as compared with males. Hence, an interaction between abuse and gender is expected. Consequently, effects of abuse on the victims will vary by gender and the difference in the delinquency referrals between abused and non-abused males will be higher than the difference for females.

Similarly, some cultural differences among different racial groups may influence the final outcomes. Different racial groups grow up in different social environments, different social conditions, and different subcultures. African-Americans often grow up with different life experiences as compared with whites. Most poor African-American youth grow up in a "survival culture" in deprived social and family conditions with much family disorganization and pathology around them. These conditions may predispose them to delinquency and crime (Glasgow, 1981 pp. 24-25). African-American children, more often than not, grow up in poor families, and disorganized neighborhoods and communities.

The negative consequences of having a "bad childhood" have been addressed by Wilson, (1987). More often than in case of whites, African-Americans live in extended families. More African-American than white children live over time with several adult care-takers. Some researchers argue that these social and family disruptions have an effect on children's behavior (Shaw and McKay, 1972; Hirschi, 1969). This may hinder the development of any strong bonds with others. In addition to weakening some bonds, a traumatic experience like physical or sexual abuse may further enhance the probabilities of weakening or severing already weakened bonds. Consequently, it is expected that the outcomes will vary by racial group and that abused African-Americans will have higher delinquency referral rates.

Severity of abuse is likely to explain the variance among abused children. Severely abused children are more likely to learn and internalize abusive behavior that they had been exposed to as compared to less severely abused children. These children may also be more likely to have weakened or severed bonds. Their experience of extreme abuse may destroy any desire to have any attachment, commitment, or belief in the adults or society in general. These children may have no personal stakes in conformity. Consequently, they may be more inclined to engage in delinquency. Based on this logic it can be hypothesized that the consequences of abuse will vary by the severity of the experience of abuse.

As discussed above, it is hypothesized that abused children are expected to differ from non-abused children in delinquency referrals. The outcomes are expected to vary by race, age, and gender. The severity of abuse is expected to explain variation in delinquency among abused children. Next, a brief synopsis of discussion and proposed research is presented.

Discussion and Proposed Research

Results of the prospective studies that have adequate comparison groups and used substantiated data provide a moderate estimate of the relationship between abuse and delinquency. Prospective design studies help estimate more precisely the magnitude of this relationship. Based on what is reviewed and discussed, it seems that the prospective longitudinal research designs, using official data along with specific Operationalization criteria, are the logical alternative to other research designs used in the past. Inclusion of adequate control groups should also be advantageous in examining the magnitude of the relationship.

This research attempts to make an improvement on the existing research by overcoming some of these problems. The proposed research uses prospective longitudinal design, officially verified data, official definitions of dependent and independent measures, and a matched control group.

Chapter 4

Child Abuse: Data and Methodology

Research Design

This study is a prospective longitudinal study that utilizes a quasi-experimental design, also referred to as a "prospective or observational cohort study" (Altemeier et al., 1979; Leventhal, 1982; Schulsinger et al., 1981; Widom, 1989a). The central hypothesis guiding this research is that child abuse is causally related to delinquency. As discussed in the previous chapter, prospective longitudinal research designs are considered the best methods of research for establishing, or at least examining, the magnitude of this relationship.

The preference for this method derives from the traditional consideration of experimental designs as the most appropriate to examine causal relationships. While the design used in this study and other prospective longitudinal designs are far from being true experiments, they borrow much of their logic from the experimental design.

The classical diagram that shows the experimental design is presented below in Figure 1. This diagram, adapted from Stouffer (1962, p. 292), shows the procedure of establishing a causal relationship through the comparison of the outcomes on dependent variables between experimental and control groups.

Experimental Group	Control Group
$Time_1$ Ye_1	Yc_1
"Cause" (X) introduced	"Cause" (X) not introduced
$Time_2$ $Ye_2 - Ye_1 = de$	$Yc_2 - Yc_1 = dc$

Figure 1: Classical Experimental Design

The key features of the classical experiment are as follows:

(1)   Two randomly selected samples: experimental (E) and control (C).
(2)   Scheduling of the experimental stimuli or a factor (X), hypothesized to be causally related with the outcome (Y), in the experimental sample but not in the control sample.
(3)   Both samples are observed during $Time_1$ and $Time_2$.

Since the subjects were randomly assigned the outcomes are not expected to differ unless the experimental stimuli (X) is causally related with the outcome (Y). The changes that occur in the control sample (dc) are then compared with the changes that occur in the experimental sample (de). The difference in the changes is attributed to the introduced factor that was hypothesized to be causal.

Stouffer (1962) explains that, "The test of whether a difference (de) is attributable to what we think it is attributable to is whether `de' is significantly larger than `dc'." Since a true experiment is performed under the full control of the researcher the results obtained through true experiments allow strong conclusions. But in most social situations true experimentation is not feasible. In such circumstances, quasi-experimental designs represent an important alternative to true experiments. Such is the case in this study. A group of abused subjects' records are examined to determine whether abuse has any relationship with the victim's involvement in delinquent behavior. It was not possible to randomly assign abuse status or control the timing of the exposure to abuse (the independent variable assumed to be causally associated with the outcome of delinquency). But it was possible to select a group of children who had experienced abuse verified by a governmental agency. It was also possible to create a matched control group of children who had come to the attention of the same agency for reasons other than abuse or delinquency.

The design utilized in this study borrows its comparative logic from the experimental design. Figure 2 outlines, in a diagram, the design I am using in this study.

Experimental Group	Control Group

"Cause" (X) present   "Cause" (X) absent

$Time_1$

$Ye_1 = 0$ $Yc_1 = 0$

$Time_2$

Ye_2 Yc_2

$$Ye_2 - Yc_2 = d$$

Figure 2: Quasi-Experimental Design For This Study

The main features of this design are as follows:

(1) Two samples an "experimental" sample of abused children (E) and a control sample of non-abused children (C), were selected.
(2) The control sample was closely matched with the experimental sample so that the subjects in both groups would be as nearly alike as possible on some of those known factors potentially affecting the outcome.
(3) The factor presumed causal, "X", occurred to the members of E but not to the members of C.
(4) The dependent variable Y, delinquency, was observed in both samples at $Time_1$ and found to be zero.
(5) Both samples were observed on the dependent variable "Y" at $Time_2$.
(6) The changes that took place in Y between $Time_1$ and $Time_2$ in the experimental sample (E) were compared with the changes that were observed in Y in the control sample (C). Since the dependent variable, delinquency, was zero at $Time_1$ in both E and C, the frequency of Y_e and Y_c represent these changes.

This design differs from the experimental design depicted in Figure 1, in that the assignment of subjects to the experimental and control samples was not done at random and the independent variable (abuse), presumed to be the cause of the outcome (delinquency), was not introduced nor was it manipulated in any way. The children in the 'experimental,' sample were chosen precisely because they had been affected by it. Nonetheless, the design used here is similar to the experimental design diagramed in Figure 1 in that the control sample was closely matched with the experimental sample to control for the extraneous variables. Both samples were observed at $Time_1$ and $Time_2$, and only sample `e' was subject to the experimental variable.

The samples are matched on several major variables that could account for the outcome. Thus, if the difference in the dependent variable (delinquency) at $Time_2$ between the experimental and control group (Ye_2 - $Yc_2 = d$) is not significant, then it will imply that abuse is not causally related to delinquency. On the other hand, a significant difference in the outcome (delinquency) between two groups would suggest a causal relationship between abuse and delinquency.

Quasi-experimental designs lack random assignment and full experimental control. Consequently the comparisons depend on nonequivalent groups that differ from each other in many ways other than the presence of a "cause" whose effect is being examined. Since full experimental control is lacking, it becomes imperative that the researcher be thoroughly aware of which specific variables his particular design fails to control. The quality of inference depends on making the irrelevant causal forces explicit (Cook and Campbell, 1979) and on the quality of matching.

Causal interpretations of the results of quasi-experiments are more tenuous than those of true experiments (Campbell and Stanley, 1963), but they are much more tenable than causal interpretations from non-experimental designs. Inferences based on quasi-experiments are tenuous because the researcher does not have full control and there may be several known, suspected or unknown variables that may affect the results. The inferences drawn are firmer than those drawn from non-experimental designs because the researcher has controlled at least some of the known or suspected correlates of the outcome and has controlled the time sequence of events. Hence, quasi-experimental designs are the best alternative when true experiments are not feasible. To summarize, the design used in this study, though not a true experiment, allows the assessment of the independent effects of the causal factor (abuse) on delinquency with reasonable safety.

Data

The sample for the abused children, who were born between January 1, 1977 and December 31, 1981 was identified through the on-line computerized data base for the Florida Protective Services System

(FPSS)[2], a system that was implemented in June 1988 for recording and investigating child abuse in Florida. The main elements of the data structure and the procedures for data gathering are discussed below.

The Population for the Study

The population from which abuse cases for this study were selected consisted of all the dependency cases[3] verified as abuse cases by FPSS's Department of Health and Rehabilitative Services (DHRS) in District Three of the state of Florida during the period January 1, 1988 through December 31, 1990--a total of 18,503 validated cases of abuse. District Three is comprised of 19 counties in North-central Florida (see Appendix A for the list of counties in District Three). Dependency cases include all kinds of abuse including but not limited to parental abuse, (the perpetrator could be a known person, e.g., parent, caretaker, teacher, or any other adult whom the child knows, or a stranger[4]) that may require the state to intervene to protect the child's interests and welfare.

Procedure for the Selection of Groups

The Abused Group

The abused group for this study includes cases of 477 children who have been physically and/or sexually abused. Some of the victims, in addition, also suffered parental or family neglect. Justification for the inclusion of cases that are reported and verified as including both abuse and neglect is that while pure cases of abuse do exist, in reality the various forms of abuse often overlap (Widom, 1989a; Besharov, 1982; Pianta et al. 1989; Cicchetti and Barnett, 1991; Zingraff et al., 1993). Children living in an abusive environment are often victims of several types of abuse simultaneously, irrespective of the type reported and substantiated. Thus, including all types of abuse in the sample is justified.

Procedure

The process of selecting the abused group for this research project began with a search of all District Three abuse cases that met the following criteria: (1) The subject had to have his/her birthday between January, 1977 and December, 1981; (2) the subject had to have experienced abuse between January 1, 1988 and December 31, 1990; and (3) the subject had to have experienced abuse on or before the age of eleven. Age of ten was decided as a cut-off point to keep the temporal sequence of the events straight. That is, delinquency must appear to be the consequence of abuse, not a cause. To keep the *abuse* occurring before *delinquency,* children abused after the age of eleven were not included. These specific criteria of year of birth, year of abuse, and the temporal sequence of abuse and delinquency, determined the number of subjects that met all the conditions. A total of 477 cases in District Three met these specific age and date criteria.

HRS Reporting, Investigation, and Verification Procedures

The Central Abuse Registry is the starting point of the FPSS continuum. All incoming reports of abuse within the state are centrally received and screened by trained FPSS abuse registry counselors. An 800-96-ABUSE hot line facilitates the reporting. Next, all reports are checked against the FPSS data base to determine if the child or the parents have any previous involvement in abuse, neglect, or exploitation investigations. Then the reports are transmitted to protective services investigators who review the report at a local terminal linked to the statewide database and begin the field investigation within 24 hours. Normally, protective services investigators make a home visit and interview the alleged victim as well as the alleged perpetrator(s). If the investigator believes the abuse report to be true, a medical examination is usually performed when such examination has not been previously performed. This specific investigation verifies the occurrence of abuse and the type of abuse. If abuse is substantiated, then this report is entered in the data base as a verified abuse case (Florida Protective Services System Annual Report, 1991:4-10).

All dependency reports investigated and validated by a social service agency are computerized according to the dates the incidents are reported and substantiated. These records are maintained as on-line information in the Client Information System file. These are complete records of the report and substantiation of abuse including residential address of the child and family, disposition of the case, and protective and social services provided to the child through the Children, Youth, and Families Services Department.

Strengths of the Data

Reliability and Validity of the Data

Much of the early research in this area is based on designs weakened by questionable accuracy of information owing to reliance on second-hand information or self-report accounts of prior abuse rather than on directly observed or validated behaviors. Often there is no medical or direct evidence of the severity, frequency, or chronicity of abuse. No attempt is made to confirm self-reported abuse through official records or personal follow-up. Verification of abuse is necessary to distinguish between the victim's recollection and perception of poor, inadequate, or improper parenting, and actual events of abuse.

Officially substantiated cases, like the ones used in this study, are more believable because the occurrence of the abuse and its major features have been observed, often over some period of time, by independent and often trained professional observers working for a government bureaucracy. This official substantiation overcomes the "interpretive and subjective problems associated with interviewing someone after the fact" (Alfaro, 1981:177).

Official records, such as the ones being used in this study, do not suffer from social desirability, retrospective recall bias, or single-perspective reporting that plague other sources of information like survey research, self-reports, and one-time parental interviews. For example, when asked to recall an incident that took place some time ago, a respondent may forget the actual incident and report it the way he or she perceived it to have happened. Or, depending on the respondent's social attitude towards abuse, he or she may restructure the incident to make it sound and look better. Thus, data collected through self-reports or survey research are often not fully believable unless the abuse incident can be independently substantiated.

Officially reported and verified abuse cases provide a solution to this problem of reliability and validity. These verified official reports convince that the incident did occur and was validated by trained professionals.

Broad Sampling Frame

In addition, official records used in this study represent the broadest possible population of validated abuse cases in the selected counties. Another possible option for obtaining samples of validated cases is court records. However, as a response to abuse incidents, court referrals are often the last resort (Zingraff et al. 1993). Most abuse cases are resolved by social services agents before reaching the courts. Therefore, cases that reach the courts are often the most extreme or the most seriously contested, or the ones HRS investigators could not resolve informally. Using court records to identify abuse cases will produce a sample including for the most part extremely severe or contested cases of abuse. Extreme abuse is not the most common abuse that occurs in the lives of average children. In addition, the effects of extremely severe abuse may be different from the effects of less severe or mild and routine kinds of abuse. For these reasons, the study of court records introduces a bias that would result in less generalizable results. Data collected from FPSS and DHRS overcome these problems to some extent. These cases were not the most severe, yet severe enough to be reported and verified by trained personnel.

Limitations of Data

Under-representation of Abuse

Although this study includes all the substantiated cases of abuse in District Three's 19 counties for the period between January 1, 1988, through December 31, 1990, it, of course, does not claim to have included all victims of abuse in this DHRS district for this period. Reported abuse and substantiated abuse are not the only abuse that take place. A great deal of abuse goes unreported and is never recorded in official social services records. In addition, reported cases are likely to involve more serious incidents and the families that social service agencies, clinicians, and the courts deal with most frequently (Groeneveld and Giovannoni, 1977; Cicchetti and Barnett, 1991; Zingraff et al., 1993).

Limitations within the Sample

Although there is evidence that abuse occurs in all social classes (Straus, Gelles, and Steinmetz, 1980), in most cases it is low-income families that are reported to and investigated by social service employees. Thus, low-income families are usually over-represented in the data collected by social service agencies (Newberger et al., 1977; Groeneveld and Giovannoni, 1977). National Incidence Study data provide information about the types of children who were abused (National Center on Child Abuse and Neglect, 1988[5]). They reveal that: (1) Females were more likely to be abused (13/1,000 compared to 8/1,000 for males), mostly because of their increased susceptibility to sexual abuse (4/1,000 versus 1/1,000); (2) The incidence of abuse increased with age, particularly for physical abuse; and (3) Impoverished children were much more likely to be abused or injured.

The effects of abuse on children from low-income families may conceivably be different in some ways from the effects of abuse on children from middle-income or high-income families. For children in low-income families, the effects of abuse may be confounded by other adverse family circumstances. Thus, delinquency observed in an abuse sample could also reflect the direct and indirect effects of lower socio-economic status (SES) as well as abuse. Consequently the use of a control group becomes very important.

Although it is necessary to use official records to avoid problems associated with brief surveys with no independent validation, because of the limitations inherent in using official case records, findings regarding the long term effects of abuse based on studies using such cases cannot be generalized to all cases of child abuse.

Limited Information

Official data are usually collected for bureaucratic purposes by functionaries. These data are not gathered for research purposes to test scientific hypotheses or to develop knowledge. These data do not have the richness of data collected through surveys or personal interviews where the researcher has examined and prepared the questions relevant to reveal the dynamics of the research problem. Thus, the scope of information and the insights these data can provide are limited. Consequently, the research questions that can be addressed using these data are limited in scope. However, these data are similar to those used in many other studies, and they do provide the basis of hypotheses for further research that can be conducted by following the identified subjects using in-depth interviews.

In spite of the noted deficiencies of the official data, identifying abused cases through officially substantiated cases has some advantages that counterbalance these weaknesses.

Potential Problems with the Sample

Following is a discussion of the limitations of the sample which should be taken into consideration in drawing conclusions.

Varying Risk at the Follow-up Periods

As described above, the subjects in the abused sample were born between January 1, 1977 to December 31, 1981 and verified as abused between January 1, 1988 to December 31, 1990. This creates situations where children born in different years have varying lengths of "at-risk" periods to be abused and varying periods to manifest the effects of abuse. For example, children born in 1977 had a shorter period to be "at-risk" of abuse but have a longer period to manifest the consequences of abuse as compared with children who are born in 1980 or 1981. These birth years, years of abuse observed, and the follow-up periods are presented in Table 1.

Table 1

Birth Years, Year Abuse Observed, and Follow-up Years

Birth Follow-up Year	Year Abuse Observed**	Age at the Time of Abuse	Age at the Time of Study	Period
1977 Yrs.	1988	10*	15-16	5
1978 Ys.	1988-1989	9-10	14-15	4-5
1979 Ys.	1988-1990	8-10	13-14	3-4
1980 Ys.	1988-1990	7-10	12-13	2-3
1981 Ys.	1988-1990	7-09	11-12	1-2

* Children born in December, 1977 turned 11 in December 1988. For example a child born on June 10, 1977 will be 10 on June 10, 1987 a

nd between January 1988 and June 1988 will still be ten and not eleven. Children who were older than eleven at the time of abuse recorded in the computerized records were excluded.

** Year of abuse observed refers to the year abuse was recorded, verified, and maintained as computerized records. The computerized records do not have data on the incidents of abuse prior to the computerization. Thus the year the first recorded incident is computerized is considered as the year of abuse observed.

These varying "at-risk" and follow-up periods, as can be seen from Table 1, present problems for the analysis. Children born in 1977 reach the age of eleven sometimes in 1988[6], depending on their date of birth. These children had only a few months to accumulate all the incidents of abuse, while a child born in 1981 has a couple of years to be abused and repeatedly abused and consequently be classified in the category of abused children.

The design used in this study helps solve this problem to some extent. Each subject in the abused group has a match in the non-abused group who is of the same age and has same length of follow-up period. Children with shorter at-risk and longer follow-up periods are compared with the children who had same length of at-risk and follow-up periods. For example a child born in 1978, abused in 1988 is matched with a child born in 1978, who came to DHRS for a variety of other services in 1988. This does not solve the problem entirely but at least presents a reasonable comparison. Unless one is conducting a pure experiment, it is very difficult not to have varying lengths of at-risk and follow-up periods. Other prospective studies (Widom, 1989a; Zingraff et al., 1993) examining the abuse-delinquency relationship have similar problems.

Risk of misclassification

Since data are collected from children born during five different years and abused in three different years, there can be a problem of measurement and Operationalization of some variables, for example frequency of abuse. A child born in 1977 had only a few months to accumulate all the incidents of abuse, while a child born in 1981 has a couple of years to be abused and repeatedly abused. This has implications for analysis. Children assumed to be the victims of only one incident of abuse might have been the victims of repeated abuse. This problem is proposed to be solved by taking only the first reported and verified incident of abuse for all the subjects as a measure of abuse and no comparisons on the outcome of delinquency referral rate based on the frequency of abuse are planned.

In addition, it is also possible that children classified as non-abused were abused prior to the years checked and we have no way of determining that. This misclassification has implications for the study, as it reduces my chances of finding significant differences between the two groups.

Another misclassification problem stems from the fact that some of the abused children may have left the state after being abused and therefore we will not find any delinquency records for them. We do not have any way of determining whether the non-existence of delinquency record is due to the child not being delinquent or leaving the state. This may deflate the delinquency referral rate among the abused. However, the same is true of the control group children. There is no reason to believe that the abused children are more likely to leave the state than the non-abused children. Consequently, control group children face the same problem.

Another measurement error that gives rise to the misclassification of delinquency referrals originates from the varying follow-up periods. Children born in 1977-78 and recorded abused in 1988 have longer follow-up periods than children born in 1981 and abused in 1990. The abused children classified as non-delinquent may not have manifested the effects of abuse as yet because they did not have a long enough follow-up period and might have become delinquent if they had a longer follow-up period. Hence, the shorter follow-up period may reduce the chances of finding significant differences.

However, as it is evident from the research reviewed , follow-up periods do not have to be necessarily long and the subjects do not have to be necessarily 15-18 years old to manifest the effects of abuse. In some studies, for example in Morse et al.'s (1970) study, subjects were five years old at the time of study and the follow-up period was three years; in Martin and Beezley's (1977) study, the subjects were seven to seventeen years old at the time of study and the follow-up period was four years; in Kinard's (1980) study, the subjects were five to twelve years old at the time of study and the follow-up period was three years; in George and Main's (1979) study, the subjects were one to three years old at the time of study and the follow-up period was one to three years; and in Wassermann and Allen's (1983) study, the subjects were fourteen month old infants at the time of study (see Chapter two for further details and more examples). As is evident from the findings of these studies and discussed earlier in chapter two and mentioned briefly in this chapter, effects of abuse do become manifest even after a short period and can be examined. This justifies our efforts to examine the effects of abuse among 12-16 year old children.

Demographic Characteristics

The subjects in the experimental study group are males and females, whites and African-Americans, who were abused at varying times of their childhood. Their demographic characteristics are presented in Table 2. White children in the sample greatly outnumber African-American children (75.8% versus 24.1%), and girls outnumber boys (63.2% versus 36.8%). At the time of the first incident of abuse, about 15.1% of the group were 7 years old, 25.4% were 8, 30.6% were 9 years old, and 28.9% were 10 years old. The mean age of the abused sample at the time of abuse was 8.7 years. This has implications for the analysis as well as the results. Since children were abused at an older age, it may be possible that the effects of abuse are not as detrimental as they would be if the subjects were abused at an earlier age.

The subjects in the abused group, at the time of study, were between eleven and sixteen years of age. Mean age at the time of study for the subjects is 13.1 years. A maximum of 5 years of follow-up period (the period between the experience of abuse and the time of the study) is possible.

Table 2
Demographic Characteristics of Abused Group

	Abused Group (N=477)	
Racial group	N	%
White	362	75.8
African-Amer.	115	24.1
Gender		
Male	176	36.8
Female	301	63.2
Age At Abuse		
7 Years	72	15.0
8 Years	121	25.4
9 Years	146	30.6
10 Years	138	28.9
Frequency of Abuse		
Only One incident	337	70.6
More than one incident	140	29.4

It may also be possible that due to the short follow-up period, the effects of abuse had not become manifest yet in some cases. A table depicting the delinquency referral rate, birth-cohort, and age at abuse is presented below. This table shows that the older the child, the higher the delinquency referral rate. Therefore, children who had longer follow-up periods have higher delinquency referral rates as compared to children with shorter follow-up periods. As discussed earlier, this finding implies that some children may be misclassified since they eventually may become delinquent. If the problem is more severe among the abused than the controls, the effect of abuse on delinquency will be smaller than in a study with longer follow-up.

Table 3

Delinquency Referral Rate by Birth-Cohort and Date of Birth

Birth-Cohort (Birth-year)	Age at Abuse (In years)	Delinquency (%)
1977 (n=24)	10	33.3
1978 (n=76)	9	12.5
	10	28.9
1979 (n=130)	8	23.8
	9	14.2
	10	14.2
1980 (n=134)	7	12.5
	8	10.0
	9	6.9
	10	13.3
1981 (n=113)	7	4.6
	8	6.2
	9	0.0

Matching Procedure and Selection of Control Group Subjects

Selection of a control group matched on as many variables as could probably intervene in the results is a critical element of this design. Control group subjects were chosen from among those children who came to the Department of Health and Rehabilitative Services (DHRS) for a variety of non-abuse services between January 1, 1988 to December 31, 1990. Only children born between January 1977 and December 1981 were included in the sample from which the matches were selected. Table 4 presents frequencies of the services provided to the control group children.

Table 4
Services Provided to the Control Group Children - Frequencies

Service Provided	Frequency
Specialized Family Services	1
Local Family Services	1
Family Shelter	3
Non-Family Shelter	2
Child Day Care	212
Refugee and Entrant Social Services	1

As is evident from Table 4, 96.3% of the abused subjects were referred to DHRS for the Child-Care Program component. The Department of Children, Youth, and Families provides Child Day Care services to families that are in need, based on income eligibility criteria. These children appear in the records for no other reason than the family's need for assistance in child-care services. The remaining 3.7% appeared in the records for the listed services which had nothing to do with reported or substantiated abuse. As discussed earlier, every possible effort was made to ascertain that these children were not referred for real or potential abuse.

Comparison group subjects were matched on the basis of gender, racial group, year of birth[7], and Zip code. Zip code was used as a rough proxy for SES. The process for selection of the matched group was relatively complex. The steps and elements that went into the process are outlined below.

Criteria for Inclusion or Exclusion in the Control Group

The Abused Group

The first requirement for a member of the control group was that the child had no report of abuse, since this study assumes that the major difference between the abused group and the control group is the experience of abuse. The subject in the control group had to be free of the "exposure." Thus, it was extremely important to assure that children selected as comparison group subjects had no history of abuse so far as it could be determined. These comparison group subjects were selected from the list of children who came to the DHRS for non-abuse services.

However, to be absolutely certain, FPSS and DHRS records for dependency between the January 1988 and December 1990 period were checked. Those children who received protective services for real or potential abuse, neglect, or delinquency in the 1988-1990 period were excluded from the sampling frame so as to create a relatively "uncontaminated" control group. None of the children used for the comparison group had been reported abused or neglected. In these protective service cases, abuse was not verified as in the cases used for the "experimental" group, but the fact that the children needed protection is indicative that child might have been abused. In spite of this precaution, we should recognize the fact that the accessible records were available in the computer for both, abused and control, groups for only between 1988 and 1990. It is possible that these control children had been abused prior to 1988. This is also true for the abused group children. This is the limitation of the data and needs to be taken into consideration when interpreting the results.

Age

The subjects in the control group had to be matched with the subjects in the abused group on several other dimensions. The subjects had to be of the same age. Age is measured and recorded in the birth year and the number of days passed in that year. The matches are found within as close a range as possible of the abused subjects. The matches were allowed to be within plus or minus 180 days of the abused subjects' age. The actual observed age differences range from 10 days to 179 days.

Racial Group and Gender

Subjects in the control group were matched on the dichotomous categories of racial group and gender with the subjects in the abused group.

Socioeconomic Status

A rough matching for socioeconomic status was also done. Zip-code areas of residence are compared and used as a rough proxy of SES. Those in the abused group came from 157 different Zip-code areas in Florida's District Three of HRS. According to "The Source book of Zip Code Demographics" (1992), the median family income in these Zip-codes ranged from $17,955 to $43,355. The vast majority (90.6%) of the Zip-codes represented in the abused sample for which family income information was available had median family incomes below the median for Florida ($30,509); 93.7% were below the median family income for the United States ($34,416). The median of the median family incomes for the abused sample was $23,000. This indicates that most of the subjects in the abused group came from the Zip-codes representing low socioeconomic status. In 73.6% of cases, an exact match for Zip code area was found. In 14.1% of the cases matches were found for the median family income of the abused subject's Zip code area family income plus or minus $1,000; in 6.9% of the cases controls were matched on the Zip code family income plus or minus $1,000 to $1,500; and in the other 5.4% of the cases SES was matched on the Zip code area family income plus or minus $2,000 to $4,000. The cases for which data were not available for the Zip codes, because these were either post office boxes or very new codes, were excluded from the sample.

However, using Zip-code areas as a proxy for SES is only a rough approximation because these are large areas. Some families with high median incomes live in lower SES Zip-code areas. Still, most of the subjects in both groups are in low-SES areas, that is most of the children in both groups have low family income. This increases the validity of the matches.

All these conditions created restrictions that limited the number of matches that could be selected. Consequently 220 matches of the abused children were attained.

Thus, there are two groups to be examined in this study - a sample of 477 abused subjects and 220 matched pairs consisting of: (a) 220 abused children from the larger group and (b) 220 matched control children who came to DHRS for services other than abuse or delinquency. The demographics of these two samples, as should be expected, are very similar. Table 5 presents a comparison of demographics of the population of abused cases with the sample of abused cases and control group subjects.

As is evident from Table 5, the abused group population has approximately similar demographic characteristics as the abused and control sample as far as racial group and gender are concerned. However, we see that the population has 5% subjects who are sixteen years old as compared with .5% in the abused group sample. Similarly we find that there are 23.7% twelve year old children in the abused group population as compared with 33.6% in the abused group sample. This tells us that the population has a higher percentage of older children as compared with the abused group sample. This will affect our results. The older children have a longer period to manifest the effects of abuse and we know from the literature that abused children have higher probability of being referred for delinquency for two reasons: age and delinquency are related; and longer follow-up increases the probability of delinquency referral. Thus, it is expected, given the demographic differences between the population and the sample, the differences between abuse and controls may be reduced.

Table 5
Comparison of Demographic Characteristics of Abused Group Population
with Abused Group and Control Group Samples

Abused Group Population (N=477)			Abused Group Sample (n=220)		Control Group Sample (n=220)	
	(n)	%	(n)	%	(n)	%
Race						
White	362	75.8	163	74.2	163	7 4 . 2
Afr-Am	115	24.1	57	25.8	57	25.8
Gender						
Male	176	36.9	80	36.4	80	3 6 . 4
Female	301	63.1	140	63.6	140	63.6
Current Age						
16 Yrs.	24	5.0	1	.5	1	.5
15 Yrs.	76	15.9	21	9.5	21	9.5
14 Yrs.	130	27.3	51	23.2	51	23.2
13 Yrs.	134	28.1	73	33.2	73	33.2
12 Yrs.	113	23.7	74	33.6	74	33.6
Age At Abuse In Years						
7	72	15.0	47	21.4		
8	121	25.4	55	25.0		
9	146	30.6	71	32.3		
10	138	28.9	47	21.4		

Operationalization of Major Constructs

A key methodological standard requires a clear description and
Operationalization of the variables so that the results of the study are
generalizable (Leventhal, 1982). The literature review on the relationship
between child abuse and delinquency has revealed that one of the factors
responsible for the current fragmented state of this research is the lack of

consensus on the definitions of dependent and independent variables. To avoid some of the ambiguity that is found in some of the previous studies, the official definition of delinquency as reported in DHRS records is treated as the dependent variable. Delinquency is viewed as an adverse outcome of the abuse incident.

A substantial number of children who engage in delinquent acts are never eligible for the official designation "delinquent" because they escape detection, and some who do not escape detection avoid the official designation because they are not adjudicated delinquent and because they have their cases dismissed before a formal petition is filed (Zingraff et al., 1993). Many children, even when detected, are diverted to community-based programs established for younger, first-time, or less serious offenders. These children fall outside the juvenile-court statistics. For these reasons, data from DHRS is more complete than data from court records.

In this study, abuse, racial group, age, gender, and SES are treated as independent variables. The severity of abuse is considered as one of the dimensions of abuse that act as stimulants or depressants in the manifestation of the adverse effects of abuse. These measures are defined and operationalized below.

Dependent Variable

Delinquency

A juvenile who had any referral to DHRS for any delinquent act is coded as delinquent. The measure of delinquency is the first delinquency referral. Each delinquent act and its disposition were recorded and coded as applicable[8]. DHRS's definitions of delinquent acts as well as dispositions of the case as described in Form (50-4) are utilized in this study to code the type of delinquency (see Appendix C). Statewide DHRS records for the time period between January 1991 to July 1993 were utilized to check for delinquency referrals for both the abused and the control group. The delinquency records for the children born in 1977, 1978, and 1979 were checked for the time period between 1989-to July 1993 (if the child turned eleven before or during 1989).The delinquent acts, the dates of such acts, the disposition of each charge, and the associated sanctions related to each charge (e.g., community control, detention, institutionalization, or community service) were recorded and coded for each subject in both groups. A maximum of 5 reported incidents of delinquency was recorded. These incidents were clustered and divided into two categories: no delinquency record and delinquency record.

Independent Variables

Abuse

As discussed earlier, any reported incident of abuse that is verified by the DHRS officials and recorded as abuse incident is considered abuse. The exact definition of abuse as provided by Chapter 415 in Florida Statute is provided in Appendix D.

Information on the type of abuse was gathered to examine the effects of different types of abuse. For example, do the consequences differ for children who have experienced physical abuse compared with those who have experienced sexual abuse? However, this information can not be used to compare the effects of one type of abuse versus another. The reason for this is that there are only 45 cases of pure physical abuse, ten cases of sexual abuse, and the rest are a combination of physical and sexual, physical, sexual, and neglect, physical and neglect. This makes any meaningful comparison difficult. Perhaps the effects of abuse differ by the type of abuse. There is empirical evidence that the victims of physical abuse engage in externalizing acts like violence (McCord, 1983) while the victims of sexual abuse may engage in internalizing acts like withdrawal and depression (Widom, 1989a). However, the issue would be difficult to examine in these data.

Racial group

The race of each subject is treated as one of the independent variables. This sample consists of African-Americans and whites. In official records a Latino person can be either white or African-American. District three has relatively few Latino families compared to other Florida districts. Based on the empirical evidence it is hypothesized that the African-Americans will have higher rate of delinquency than Whites.

Gender

The gender of each subject is treated as one of the independent variables. Both self-report and official measures of delinquency indicate that, in general, males have a higher prevalence and incidence rates than females, especially for more serious offenses (Elliott et al., 1989). Literature on crime and delinquency leads us to hypothesize that females will have lower delinquency rates than males within the abused group.

Current Age

Subjects are divided into subgroups based on the subject's current age. There are four age categories: (a) eleven and half to twelve years old; (b) thirteen years old; © fourteen years old; (d) fifteen and sixteen years old[9]. This gives the subgroups more similar periods in the abuse window than the whole sample and allows us to examine if the different lengths of follow-up periods have any effect on the outcome.

Previous research (both from official statistics and self-reports) indicates that there is a statistically significant positive relationship between age and the occurrence of delinquent acts, at least throughout the adolescent years (Elliot et al., 1989; Hirschi and Gottfredson, 1983). Based on this logic and empirical evidence, it is hypothesized that older children are more likely to appear in official data on delinquency referrals.

Severity of Abuse

Although, as mentioned earlier, all of the cases used in this study are relatively serious cases of abuse, a distinction can be made between serious and less serious abuse by the type of injury sustained during the abuse incident. Data on the type of injury were recorded and coded as applicable. Each injury was coded as defined by the DHRS. All injuries that resulted in serious physical harm have been operationalized as severe abuse. Thus, severe abuse included all physical injuries except bruises/welts, cuts/punctures, wounds/bite marks. Other injuries where the physical harm incurred is not specified are not considered severe abuse. List of these injuries is presented in the Appendix E. Next chapter presents hypotheses to be tested in this work .

Chapter 5

Hypotheses

The following are the specific hypotheses that will be addressed in the empirical analysis. The lack of specificity of some of them reflects the state of theoretical development on the relationship between child abuse and delinquency, particularly as it relates to the conditions under which abuse contributes to delinquency.

Based on the empirical evidence, the following hypotheses are formed for analysis. These are divided into two sections: (1) Hypotheses for between group analyses; and (2) Hypotheses for within group analyses. Within each section, the hypotheses are organized going from the straightforward to the more complex and two subsections are created. Subsection A presents the basic hypotheses of comparison between the abused and control groups; and subsection B presents hypotheses in regard to the combined effects of abuse, gender, age and racial group. The same pattern is followed for within group analyses.

Hypotheses for Between Group Analyses

A. Basic hypotheses

> Hypothesis # 1: The abused group is hypothesized to have a higher delinquency referral rate as compared with the delinquency referral rate of the control group.

The literature on the relationship between child abuse and juvenile delinquency, as we have seen, leads us to assume significant differences in the occurrence of delinquency among the abused and the non-abused children. Based on the research examined in the literature review, one would predict that the experience of abuse would correlate positively and highly with the incidence of delinquency. Conceptually, it could be that the experience of abuse provides a socialization framework which guides the victims' perceptions in the future making them more prone to react in ways similar to the ways in which they themselves were abusively treated. Early exposure to a harsh and punitive parental figure or repeated abuse from a close adult may affect the child's behavior through weakening or severing other social bonds. It could be that the children start believing that abuse is an appropriate, or the only appropriate, mode of interaction. The victims might internalize and adopt that mode of social interaction as their own.

Other outcomes of the experience of abuse are also possible. The victims may be so wounded in their self-esteem and autonomy that they lose even the initiative needed to engage in delinquent acts. Therefore, it can be hypothesized that delinquency among the abused subjects will be similar or lower than the control group. Furthermore, some of the studies (see Elmer, 1977; Pelton, 1978) suggest that the effects of abuse appear to be indistinguishable from those of economic deprivation. There is a real possibility that the effects of abuse might not be much different from those of being reared in an economically deprived family and community setting.

Circumstances such as poverty and the correlates of poverty may have as adverse an effect on the child as abuse. The design used in this work attempts to control for the effects such as those of poverty by having a control group approximately matched on social class. If the sample group of the abused children has a delinquency referral rate significantly higher than the control group sample, then I will say that a causal relationship exists between abuse and subsequent juvenile delinquency.

B. Combined effects hypotheses

> Hypothesis # 2: Gender: The difference between the abused and control groups in delinquency referral rate will be higher for males than for females.

Here the basic hypothesis is that gender contributes to the effect that abuse has on the subsequent delinquency referral rate and the abused males will have a higher rate than control males and abused females will have a higher rate than control females. Thus, it is expected that the difference between the abused and the control males will be higher than the difference between the abused and control females. This hypothesis is based on the notion that males are socialized to be active, aggressive, and stand up for their rights. These socialization norms would make them more inclined to engage in an externalizing behavior like delinquency, in general. The experience of abuse may further weaken their bonds with society and provoke them further to take action and engage in delinquent acts. The experience of abuse increases the vulnerability of the already "at-risk" male group. In contrast, females are socialized to be submissive, dependent, tolerant, and suppress anger. So, in general, one would expect a lower delinquency referral rate among females in both groups. However, a traumatic experience like abuse may trigger their suppressed anger and make them indulge in delinquency, which otherwise they would not. Thus, the abused females are expected to have a higher rate of delinquency than control females. However, this difference is expected to be smaller than the difference among males.

> Hypothesis # 3: Race: The difference between the abused and control groups in delinquency referral rate will be higher for the African-Americans than for the whites.

In general, there are differences by race in the official arrest records. African-Americans are referred and arrested more often (Hindelang et al., 1981) than whites. Here, our hypothesis is that race contributes to the effect that abuse has on the subsequent delinquency referral rate and the abused African-Americans will have a higher delinquency rate than the control African-Americans and the abused whites will have a higher rate than the control whites. Thus, it is expected that the difference between the abused and the control African-Americans will be higher than the difference between the abused and the control whites. The direction of the hypothesis implies that the experience of abuse is likely to increase the vulnerability of the already "at-risk" African-American group.

> Hypothesis # 4: Age: The difference between the abused and control groups in delinquency referral rate will be higher for the older than for the younger subjects.

Age has been found to be positively associated with delinquency, in general. Reports of studies by Elliot et al. (1989) and Hirschi and Gottfredson (1983) lead us to postulate that the older subjects are more likely to be found delinquent than the younger subjects. Since the abused and control group subjects are matched on age, their delinquency referral rates should not differ. Any difference in their delinquency referral rate in the different age category groups can be attributed to abuse.

It is conceptualized that learning takes place through modeling and reinforcement. This learning process is much more complicated than direct and immediate imitation like seeing and doing. The longer time period between the experience of abuse and the subjects' present age enhances their opportunities to succeed in modeling and adapting the behavior. Unless some intervention takes place, as the age increases the likelihood of the modelled behavior being reinforced also increases. This longer time period may also contribute to severing the already weakened bonds and thus leaving the subjects at the crossroads where they are more likely than not to engage in delinquency if the right opportunities arise. Thus, it is hypothesized that the difference between the abused and the control older subjects will be higher than the difference between the abused and the control younger subjects.

These four basic hypotheses about the comparison of abused and control group subjects address the main differences between the abused and control group. Based on the literature review, it can be inferred that the effects of abuse may be compounded by the combined effect of gender and racial group.

The original plan was to develop hypotheses for all combined effects. However, the categories of race and gender combined give cells with such small frequencies that such a plan was rendered infeasible and of not much use for the purposes of analysis and drawing conclusions.

Hypotheses one through four deal with the comparison of the abused and non-abused groups on delinquency and address the question "Does abuse have any causal relationship with delinquency?"

Hypotheses for Within Group Analyses

A. Basic hypotheses

Hypotheses five through eleven examine the predictors of delinquency among the population of 477 abused children for whom we also have the information on delinquency.

In these hypotheses, the variable of severity of abuse - which is hypothesized to be one circumstance affecting the outcome of delinquency referral - is added. The severity of abuse was operationalized as the extent of physical harm or injury sustained by abuse.

> Hypothesis # 5: Severity: Subjects who have been the victims of severe abuse are hypothesized to have a higher delinquency referral rate than the subjects who experienced less severe abuse.

Geller and Ford-Somma (1984) report that the victims of severe[10] abuse were more likely to be violent than the victims of mild abuse. Based on the literature, it can be expected that the victims of severe abuse are more likely to internalize their experience and adopt an abusive mode of behavior than the victims of less severe abuse. Extreme severe abuse may also act as a stimulant to trigger suppressed anger. The victim may be able to endure mild abuse and condone the abuser but not so with severe abuse. The incidence of severe abuse may contribute in making the victims lose any belief or commitment toward the adults which in turn may weaken their attachment and sever bonds. The victims may feel that they have no stake in conformity. This will enhance their prospects of engaging in delinquency.

Hypothesis # 6: Race: Within the abused population, African-Americans are expected to have a greater delinquency referral rates than whites.

As discussed in hypothesis 4, official statistics show that whites are less likely than African-Americans to be reported or arrested for delinquent acts (Hindelang et al., 1981). On the other hand, self-report studies (surveys) indicate no significant variation in delinquency by racial group (Elliott et al., 1989). Since data for my study are from official records, it is expected that the results will differ by racial group. The abused African-Americans are hypothesized to have more delinquency referrals than the abused whites. This hypothesis derives support from the literature. Widom (1989a, b, and c) found that African-Americans, in general, had higher delinquency and crime records.

Hypothesis # 7: Gender: Within the abused population, males are expected to have a greater delinquency referral rate than females.

Males within the abused population are expected to have a higher delinquency referral rate than the females in the abused population. Gender is a standard predictor of delinquency. As discussed earlier, there is empirical evidence that males are more likely to be referred and arrested for delinquency than females. Since these data are official records, differences within these groups may be even more evident because males tend to appear more often in official records than do females. This could be due to the United States society's gendered socialization norms as well as biases in social control or the agencies' mode of processing. The differences in their delinquency may be a reflection of our social norms as well.

Hypothesis # 8: Age: Within the abused population, the older subjects are expected to have a greater delinquency referral rate than the younger subjects.

Age is found to be positively associated with delinquency, in general. Reports of studies by Elliot et al. (1989) and Hirschi and Gottfredson (1983) lead us to postulate that age is one of the general predictors of delinquency and older subjects are more likely to be found delinquent than younger subjects.

The differences in delinquency referrals between the older and younger subjects could be attributed to two sources: (1) aging, in general, may increase the gap; and (2) the longer follow-up periods for the older children may increase the probability of a higher difference.

B. Combined effects hypotheses

Hypothesis # 9: Severity-Gender: Within the abused population, the effect of severity is greater for males than for females.

Earlier, we discussed that the severity of abuse and gender are associated with delinquency. Now, we hypothesize that the combination of severity and being male increases the risk of delinquency involvement.

Hypothesis # 10: Severity-Race: Within the abused population, the effect of severity is greater for African-Americans than for whites.

The severely abused African-Americans are hypothesized to have the highest delinquency referral rate. There is no clear indication in the literature as to how the severity of abuse may affect different racial groups. However, since the severity of the experience of abuse and race are considered to be the risk factors enhancing the probability of the victim's involvement in delinquency as discussed above, it is hypothesized that severity and race combined will further enhance the probability of such an outcome.

Hypothesis # 11: Race-Gender: Within the abused population, the effects of race on delinquency are greater for males than for females.

As noted above, African-Americans, in general, have higher arrest records, which leads us to hypothesize higher rates for both genders among African-Americans. Out of these two subgroups, the abused African-American males, in particular, are expected to have the highest delinquency records. Some of the earlier studies (Widom, 1989c) found abused African-American males to be at higher risk of delinquency than the abused African-American females, abused white males, and abused white females. The next chapter discusses procedures for the proposed analysis.

Chapter 6

Procedures

Proposed Analyses

As discussed earlier, delinquency status is a dependent variable. In this study, there are two different sets of data (1)a sample of 220 abused subjects with a matched control sample and (2) a population of 477 abused subjects, a group that includes the 220 experimental subjects that have matched pairs and 257 that could not be matched. Thus, this work will engage in two different kinds of analyses: (1) between group analyses comparing a sample of 220 abused group subjects with 220 control group subjects; and (2) within group analyses using the population of 477 abused subjects. We begin with the discussion of the analytical techniques that are used in the between group analyses. It is followed by a discussion of the techniques used in the within group analyses.

Procedures for Between Group Analysis

First, the abused and control groups are compared. Descriptive statistics are expected to yield the distribution of delinquency status in the experimental and control groups and within these the same distribution among the race, gender, and severity subgroups that the hypotheses require. Next, the binomial approach to McNemar's test will be applied to compare the abused and control groups. Fisher's Exact test will also be used to examine differences in the effect of abuse between subgroups.

McNemar's Test.

In order to examine the effect of abuse on delinquency, cross-classification 2x2 tables are created. Each of these tables has four cells cross-classifying delinquent and non-delinquent members of the pairs. An abstract model of the cross-classification table is provided in figure 3.

Actual tables used to compute McNemar's test using the binomial approach are presented as part of the respective analyses.

		Non-abused member of the pair	
		Delinquent (+)	NotDelinquent(-)
Delinq. (+)		p++ cell "a"	p + -
cell "b" Abused member of the pair			
Not Delinq. (-)		p-+ cell "c"	p-- cell "d"
		p++ + p+- + p-+ + p-- = 1	

Figure 3:   Model for Cross-classification Table of Abused and Non-abused Subjects.

If both members of the matched pair are delinquent, the pair contributes to the proportion of the upper left cell of the table. If neither is delinquent, they go in the lower right cell. In general, one expects that if one member of a pair is delinquent, the other one has a high probability of being delinquent because they are matched on some variables that are related to delinquency, such as, gender, race, socioeconomic status and age. To apply the binomial approach to McNemar's test, the off-diagonal cells "b" and "c" are used. Here, n = sum of the off diagonal cells "b" and "c", X = cell "b", and p = .5 (Agresti and Finlay, 1986: 187-188).

The idea behind this test is that, cells "a" and "d" are shared by abused and non-abused--they indicate the numbers of persons who are delinquent and not delinquent in both groups. The only way abuse can have an effect on delinquency is if cell "b" is greater than cell "c". McNemar's test allows us to examine whether cell "b" is significantly different from cell "c". When some of the off-diagonal cells are less than five, like the ones in this study, it is necessary to use the binomial approach to McNemar's test to test the hypothesis (Agresti and Finlay, 1986:188).

The Binomial Test

The formula for the probabilities of a binomial distribution (Agresti and Finlay, 1986:143) is :

$$P(X) = \frac{n!}{X!(n-X)!} \prod\nolimits^{x} (1-\prod)^{n-x}$$

For McNemar's test, n = the sum of off-diagonal cells of the cross-classification table, X = the number in cell `b' and $\prod$ = .5 (Agresti and Finlay, 1986:188). To get the probability of a result this extreme or more extreme, one must sum the probability of X given n and the probabilities of results more extreme, given n (Agresti and Finlay, 1986:143-144).

Fisher's Exact Test

We also would like to examine the hypothesis that the effect of abuse varies across categories of age, race, and gender. The Fisher's exact test is the "appropriate small sample test" (Agresti and Finlay, 1986).

Similar tables like those in Figure 3 showing the delinquent and non-delinquent matched members of the subgroups --for example, males and females, whites and African-Americans, twelve and thirteen year olds and fourteen and fifteen year olds are presented to run Fisher's Exact test.

In the cross-classification table, cells "a" and "d" are shared by abused and non-abused--they indicate the numbers of persons who are delinquent and not delinquent in both groups. The only way abuse can have an effect on delinquency is if cell "b" is greater than cell "c". Fisher's exact test allows us to examine whether the relative size of category "b" compared to "c" is greater in one group than in another. In other words, the Fisher's exact test which is applied to the tables built on the abstract model in Figure 4 will test whether the effect of abuse on delinquency is the same in the two groups. An abstract model of these tables is provided in Figure 4.

	Subgroup 1	Subgroup 2
Abused= delinquent/non-abused=not delinquent	p+- cell "a"	p+- cell " b "
A+B		
Abused=not delinquent/ not abused=delinquent	p-+ cell "c"	p-+ cell "d"
C+D		
A+C	B+D	

Figure 4: Contingency Table Displaying Delinquency Status.

The Fisher's exact test is a substitute for the Chi-square test (which is discussed under within group analysis) for small samples. The formula for Fisher's exact test (Siegel, 1956:97), based on the cells of Figure 4 is:

$$p= (A+B)! \ (C+D)! \ (A+C)! \ (B+D)!/N!A!B!C!D!$$

To determine the probability of a given table or one more extreme, one must compute Fisher's exact test for the more extreme tables and sum the probabilities (Siegel, 1956:98-99).

Procedures for Within Group Analyses

For within group analyses, we begin with cross-classification tables. Cross-classification tables are often useful in detecting relationships between two categorical variables (Agresti and Finlay, 1986:208-212). These variables are "statistically independent if the population conditional distributions on one of them are identical for each of the levels of the other.

Variables are <u>statistically dependent</u> if the conditional distributions are not identical" (Agresti and Finlay, 1986:202).

The chi-square test is based on a comparison between the frequencies that are observed in the cells of the cross-classification table and those that we would expect to observe if the null hypothesis of independence were true. The test statistic for the test of independence helps to summarize how close the expected frequencies are to the observed frequencies. The level of significance for accepting the hypothesis is set at .10. "The form of the test statistic, symbolized by χ^2 and referred to as the (Pearson) **Chi-square statistic,"** (Agresti and Finlay, 1986:204) is:

$$\chi^2 = \sum \frac{(f_o - f_e)^2}{f_e}$$

"where f_e = (row total)(column total) / total sample size" (Agresti and Finlay, 1986:209). The P value equals the right hand tail area beyond the observed χ^2 value, for a chi-square distribution with the degrees of freedom $(r-1)(c-1)$ (Agresti and Finlay, 1986:205).

The selected level of significance is the measure of the extent of evidence about H_o and H_a. The smaller the p-value, the more contradictory the data are to H_o because a smaller p-value implies that if H_o were true, it would be unusual to observe data such as those actually observed (Agresti and Finlay, 1986:148-149). Usually, levels of significance between .01 to .10 are the standard landmarks for the rejection or not rejection of the hypothesis. Levels of significance determine the probability of Type I (rejecting H_o when it is true) and Type II error (not rejecting H_o when it is false). The smaller the level of significance, "the larger the probability of Type II error for a particular alternative value, and vice versa" (Agresti and Finlay, 1986:150). We decided to use .10 as our criteria to reject our hypothesis. Although the set level of significance increases the probability of Type I error ("false positive" results), this risk is appropriate since my goal is to "scan a number of hypotheses to see which might warrant further investigation" (Agresti and Finlay, 1986). We will reject our H_o at α-level if $P < \alpha$ and will use non-directional (two-tail) tests.

However, the value of χ^2 statistic depends on the sample size and the amount of departure from independence for the two variables (Agresti and Finlay, 1986:208). Larger samples will yield significant Chi-square values despite a weak association between the two variables (Agresti and Finlay,

1986:208-209). So, one must take that into consideration when drawing
conclusions based on this statistic.

In addition, the standard Chi-square test assumes the independence of the
observations. The test is appropriate for independent samples when the
observations are independent of each other, for example, within group
analysis in this study. When the samples are dependent, as is the case in
between group analysis, the chi-square is not appropriate as it is not
sensitive to the dependent nature of the observations (Agresti and Finlay,
1986).

Logistic Regression

Although the standard Chi-square test is appropriate for the within group
analysis (477 independent cases), it does not test some of the specific
interaction hypotheses. To test these specific hypotheses, simple logistic
regression analysis will be utilized. For dichotomous dependent variables,
logistic regression allows us to model how the proportion of responses in
one of the two categories depends on independent variables. This can be
explained by the formula $\log \{\prod/1\text{-}\prod\} = \alpha + ßX$ (Agresti and Finlay,
1986:483).   "The function $\log [\prod/(1\text{-}\prod)]$ is called the logistic
transformation (or logit) and this model is referred to as a logistic
regression model. It is standard to use natural logs (base e) in logistic
models. As $\prod$ increases from 0 to 1, the logit increases from $-\infty$ to ∞.
The probability $\prod = 1/2$ corresponds to a logit of 0, and $\prod$ values above
(below) ½ correspond to positive (negative) logits. If $ß = 0$ in the logistic
model, the logit (and hence $\prod$) does not change as X changes. . . . For
positive ß, $\prod$ increases as X increases. For negative ß, $\prod$ decreases as X
increases; in other words, the probability of a '1' response tends toward 0
for larger values of X" (Agresti and Finlay, 1986: 483).

"Let $\prod = E(Y)$ denote the proportion of '1' responses in the population.
Now $\prod$ also represents the probability that a randomly selected subject
makes the response '1' and this probability may vary according to the
values of the independent variables" (Agresti and Finlay, 1986:482). This
model is described in the following equation: $\ln(p/1\text{-}p) = a + b*X + b*Y + b*X*Y$ (Agresti and Finlay, 1986:485-486).

The logistic regression model is used to examine the interaction effects,
for example, males and females. It is appropriate to use logistic regression
when the dependent variable is a simple dichotomy (Agresti and Finlay,
1986).

Chapter 7

Analysis

In this chapter, two different kinds of analyses are presented. The first section explores the differences in delinquency referrals between abused and non-abused children in 220 pairs matched as described in chapter 4. As explained earlier these are called "Between Group Analyses." The second section examines the variables that may explain the variation in delinquency within the larger group of 477 abused children. These are called "Within Group Analyses."

Section 1

Between Group Analysis

Earlier it was hypothesized that the experience of abuse would cause differences in delinquency referral rates. For purposes of clarity of exposition the hypotheses are reproduced below. As discussed earlier, delinquency was operationalized as any complaint against the juvenile that was reported to and recorded by DHRS as a referral. This variable was coded "1" to indicate the presence of a referral and "0" to indicate the absence of a referral. A referral means the child has a record for having been referred for delinquent action[11] and "no referral" means the child was not recorded as having been referred for delinquent action.

A. Basic hypotheses

Hypothesis # 1: The abused group is hypothesized to have a higher delinquency referral rate as compared with the delinquency referral rate of the control group.

The comparison of the percentages of delinquency referral rates between both groups presented in Table 6, as hypothesized, indicates that the abused group has a higher delinquency referral rate than the control group.

Table 6

Delinquency Referral Rates of Abused and Control Groups - Percentages

Abused (n=220)	Controls (n=220)	
Difference		
10.0	6.4	3.6

The referral rate for the abused group is 56% higher than for the control group. However, we do not know whether the difference is significant given the small numbers involved. Large differences involving small numbers are not necessarily significant and do not produce stable results from one sample to the next. Thus, to examine the significance of the difference in delinquency referral rate between the abused and control groups, we decided to use *the McNemar's test using the binomial approach*. The results for the comparison of the abused and control groups, are presented in Table 7a-b. The computations and the formula used to compute the binomial test are presented in Table 7a.

Table 7a
Cross-classification Table for Abused and Non-abused subjects
        Non-abused member of the pair

		Delinquent (+)	NotDelinquent(-)
	Delinq. (+)	p++	p + -
		12	10
Abused member of the pair		p-+	p -
Not Delinq. (-)		2	196

Table 7b
Binomial Test Results for the Comparison of Abused and Control Groups

H_o: $\prod = .5$
$\quad\quad n = 12$
$p(X_{12} \geq 10) = \sum_{10} [12] (.5)^{12}$

$P(X_{12} \geq 10) = [12] (.5)^{12} + [12] (.5)^{12} + [12] (.5)^{12}$
$\quad\quad\quad\quad\quad\quad 10 \quad\quad\quad\quad 11 \quad\quad\quad\quad 12$

$$= \frac{12!}{10!2!} (.5)^{12} + \frac{12!}{11!1!} (.5)^{12} + \frac{12!}{12!0!} (.5)^{12}$$

$$= (66 + 12 + 1)(.5)^{12}$$

$$= 79(.5)^{12}$$
$$= 79(.00024414)$$
$$= .0192 \text{ (one-sided prob.)}$$
$$= .0192(2)$$
$$= .0384 \text{(two-sided exact p-value)}.$$
Binomial test P=.0192 (one-sided)
$\quad\quad\quad\quad$ P=.0384 (two-sided)

The results of the binomial test show that abuse is related to delinquency and of the pairs, abused subjects are more likely to be referred for delinquency. This is found significant at the .038 level. This is evidence against the null hypothesis of no difference and evidence in support of my research hypothesis as stated. Thus, the null hypothesis of no relationship is rejected and the research hypothesis as stated, is accepted.

B. Combined effects hypotheses

Hypothesis # 2: Gender: The difference between the abused and control groups in delinquency referral rate will be higher for males than for females.

Table 8 provides results on the differences in delinquency referral rates between abused and control males, abused and control females. The binomial approach to McNemar's test is used to compare abused males with non-abused males and abused females with non-abused females.

Fisher's Exact test is used to compare males and females. The results of the comparison between abused and controls by gender are presented in Table 8-8e.

Table 8
Comparison of Delinquency Referral Rates Between Abused and Control Subjects by Gender - Proportions

| | Abused | Controls | |
| | (n=220) | (n=220) | |
			Diff.
Males (n=80)	.175	.099	.076
Females (n=140)	.057	.043	.014

Table 8a
Cross-classification Table for Abused and Non-abused Males

| | | Non-abused member of the pair | |
	Delinquent (+)		NotDelinquent(-)
Abused member of the pair	Delinq. (+)	p++ 8	p + - 6
	Not Delinq. (-)	p-+ 0	p-- 66
			n=80

Table 8b
Binomial Test Results for the Comparison of Abused and Control Males

$H_o: \prod = .5$

$n = 6$

$$p(X_6 \geq 6) = \Sigma \ [6] \ (.5)^6$$
$$\quad\quad\quad\quad\quad\quad 6$$

$$P(X_6 \geq 6) = \ [6] \ (.5)^6$$
$$\quad\quad\quad\quad\quad\quad 6$$

$$= \frac{6!}{6!0!} \ (.5)^6$$

$$= (1)(.5)^6$$
$$= (1)(.0156)$$
$$= .0156 \ \text{(one-sided prob.)}$$
$$= .0156 \ (2)$$
$$= .0312 \ \text{(two-sided exact p-value)}.$$

Binomial test P=.0156 (one-sided)
P=.0312 (two-sided)

Table 8c
Cross-classification Table for Abused and Non-abused Females

		Non-abused member of the pair	
		Delinquent (+)	NotDelinquent(-)
	Delinq. (+)	p++ 4	p + - 4
Abused member of the pair			
	Not Delinq. (-)	p-+ 2	p-- 1 3 0
			n=140

Table 8d

Binomial test Results for the Comparison of Abused and Control Females

H_o: $\prod = .5$

$n = 6$

$p(X_6 \geq 4) = \Sigma \begin{bmatrix} 6 \\ 4 \end{bmatrix} \begin{bmatrix} 6 \\ 5 \end{bmatrix} \begin{bmatrix} 6 \\ 6 \end{bmatrix} (.5)^6$

$P(X_6 \geq 4) = \begin{bmatrix} 6 \\ 4 \end{bmatrix} \begin{bmatrix} 6 \\ 5 \end{bmatrix} \begin{bmatrix} 6 \\ 6 \end{bmatrix} (.5)^6$

$$= \frac{6!}{4!2!} (.5)^6 + \frac{6!}{5!1!} (.5)^6 + \frac{6!}{6!0!} (.5)^6$$

$= (15+6+1)(.5)^6$

$= (22)(.0156)$

$= .343$ (one-sided prob.)

$= .343$ (2)

$= .686$ (two-sided exact p-value).

Binomial test P=.343 (one-sided)

P=.686 (two-sided)

Table 8e
Off-Diagonal Cells from Table 8a and Table 8b for Fisher's Exact Test

	Males	Females
Abused= delinquent/non- abused=not delinquent	p+- 6	p+- 4
Abused=not delinquent/ not abused=delinquent	p-+ 0	p-+ 2
Fisher's Exact Test (Left)	1.000	
(Right)	0.227	
(2-Tail)	0.455	

The delinquency referral rate among the abused males is 76% higher than the control males. The delinquency referral rate among the abused females is 32.5% higher than the control females. However, as discussed earlier, these large differences may not be necessarily significant given the small numbers involved because they do not take into account sampling variability in a small sample. Consequently, large differences involving small numbers do not produce stable results from one sample to the next. To examine the significance of the difference, we decided to use the binomial approach to McNemar's test. As can be seen the binomial approach to McNemar's test for males shows the p-value of .031 and for females .686. Fisher's exact test yields a p-value of .455. Although the abused males have significantly higher delinquency referral rate, the tests for the difference between abused and control females do not yield desirable significance. The Fisher's exact test for the comparison between males and females does not yield a significance level required to accept the research hypothesis. So we reject the research hypothesis as stated.

> Hypothesis # 3: Race: The difference between the abused and control groups in delinquency referral rate will be higher for the African-Americans than for the whites.

The comparison of the proportions of delinquency referral rate between the abused and control groups indicates that the abused African-Americans have a higher rate of delinquency referrals than the abused whites. The results of the binomial test and Fisher's Exact test are presented in Table 9-9e.

Table 9
Comparison of Delinquency Referral Rates Between Abused and Control Subjects by Race - Proportions

	Abused (n=220)	Controls (n=220)	Difference
African-Americans (n=57)	.122	.070	. 0 5 2
Whites (n=163)	.092	.061	. 0 3 1

Table 9a
Cross-classification Table for Abused and Non-abused Whites

| | Non-abused member of the pair | |
	Delinquent (+)	NotDelinquent(-)
Delinq. (+)	p++ 8	p + - 7
Abused member of the pair		
Not Delinq. (-)	p-+ 2	p-- 146 n=163

Table 9b
Binomial test Results for the Comparison of Abused and Control Whites

$H_o: \prod = .5$

$n = 9$

$$p(X_9 \geq 7) = \Sigma \begin{bmatrix} 9 \\ 7 \end{bmatrix} \begin{bmatrix} 9 \\ 8 \end{bmatrix} \begin{bmatrix} 9 \\ 9 \end{bmatrix} (.5)^9$$

$$P(X_9 \geq 7) = \begin{bmatrix} 9 \\ 7 \end{bmatrix} \begin{bmatrix} 9 \\ 8 \end{bmatrix} \begin{bmatrix} 9 \\ 9 \end{bmatrix} (.5)^6$$

$$= \frac{9!}{7!2!} (.5)^9 + \frac{9!}{8!1!}(.5)^9 + \frac{9!}{9!0!}(.5)^9$$

$= (36+9+1)(.5)^9$

$= (46)(.00195)$

$= .0898$ (one-sided prob.)

$= .0898$ (2)

$= .1796$ (two-sided exact p-value).

Binomial test P=.089 (one-sided)

P=.179 (two-sided)

Table 9c
Cross-classification Table for Abused and Non-abused African-Americans

	Non-abused member of the pair	
	Delinquent (+)	NotDelinquent(-)
Delinq. (+) Abused member of the pair	p++ 4	p + - 3
Not Delinq. (-)	p-+ 0	p-- 50 n=57

Table 9d
Binomial test Results for the Comparison of Abused and Control African-Americans

H_o: $\prod = .5$
$n = 3$
$p(X_3 \geq 3) = \Sigma [3] (.5)^3$
                    3

$P(X_3 \geq 3) = [3](.5)^3$
                      3

$= \dfrac{3!}{3!} (.5)^3$

        $= (1)(.5)^3$
        $= (1)(.125)$
        $= .125$ (one-sided prob.)
        $= .125 (2)$
        $= .250$ (two-sided exact p-value).
Binomial test P=.125 (one-sided)
              P=.250 (two-sided)

Table 9e
Off-diagonal Cells form Table 9a and Table 9b for Fisher's Exact Test

	Whites	African-Americans
Abused= delinquent/non-abused=not delinquent	p+- 7	p+- 3
Abused=not delinquent/ not abused=delinquent	p-+ 2	p-+ 0

Fisher's Exact Test (Left)	0.545
(Right)	1.000
(2-Tail)	1.000

Table 9-9e show that the effects of abuse vary by racial group. The delinquency rate among abused African-Americans is 75% higher than that of control African-Americans. The delinquency rate among the abused whites is 50% higher than the control whites. These observed large differences may not be statistically significant because of the small numbers involved. The binomial approach to McNemar's Chi-square statistic yields a p-value of .25 for African-Americans and .179 for whites. Fisher's exact test yields p-value of 1.00. This is evidence against our research hypothesis. Therefore, we reject the research hypothesis as stated.

Hypothesis # 4: Age: The difference between the abused and control groups in delinquency referral rate will be higher for the older than for the younger subjects.

To test this hypothesis, both abused and control groups are compared on the basis of the subjects' current age. These results are presented in Table 10-10g.

Table 10
Comparison of Delinquency Referral Rates Between Abused and Control Subjects by Age - Proportions

	Abused (n=220)	Controls (n=220)	Difference	
12 Years Old	.042	.042	.00	(n=74)
13 Years Old	.068	.068	.00	(n=73)
14 Years Old	.160	.059	.101	(n=51)
15 Years Old	.238	.143	.095	(n=21)

Table 10a
Cross-classification Table for Abused and Non-abused Twelve Year Olds

	Non-abused member of the pair	
	Delinquent (+)	Not Delinquent (-)
Delinq. (+)	p++ 3	p+- 0
Abused member of the pair		
Not Delinq. (-)	p-+ 0	p-- 71
		n=74

Table 10b

Cross-classification Table for Abused and Non-abused Thirteen Year Olds

Non-abused member of the pair

	Delinquent (+)	Not Delinquent (-)
Delinq. (+)	p++ 3	p+- 2

Abused member
of the pair

	Delinquent (+)	Not Delinquent (-)
Not Delinq. (-)	p-+ 2	p-- 67
		n=74

Table 10c
Cross-classification Table for Abused and Non-abused Fourteen Year Olds

Non-abused member of the pair

	Delinquent (+)	Not Delinquent (-)
Delinq. (+)	p++ 3	p+- 5

Abused member
of the pair

	Delinquent (+)	Not Delinquent (-)
Not Delinq. (-)	p-+ 0	p-- 43
		n=51

Table 10d
Binomial Test Results for the Comparison of Abused and Control Fourteen Year Olds

H_o: $\prod = .5$
$n = 5$
$p(X_5 \geq 5) = \sum [5] (.5)^5$
$\qquad\qquad\quad 5$

$P(X_5 \geq 5) = \dfrac{[5](.5)^5}{5}$

$= \dfrac{5!}{5!} (.5)^5$

$= (1)(.5)^5$
$= (1)(.031)$
$= .031$ (one-sided prob.)
$= .031 (2)$
$= .062$ (two-sided exact p-value).
Binomial test P=.031 (one-sided)
$\qquad\qquad$ P=.062 (two-sided)

Table 10e
Cross-classification Table for Abused and Non-abused Fifteen Year Olds

| | Non-abused member of the pair | |
	Delinquent (+)	Not Delinquent (-)
Delinq. (+)	p++ 3	p+- 3
Abused member of the pair		
Not Delinq. (-) n=21	p-+ 0	p-- 16

Table 10f
Binomial Test Results for the Comparison of Abused and Control Fifteen
Year Olds

H_o: $\prod$ = .5
n = 3
$p(X_3 \geq 3) = \Sigma [3] (.5)^3$
            3

$P(X_3 \geq 3) = [3](.5)^3$
            3

$$= \frac{3!}{3!} (.5)^3$$

= $(1)(.5)^3$
= (1)(.125)
= .125 (one-sided prob.)
= .125 (2)
= .250 (two-sided exact p-value).
Binomial test P=.125 (one-sided)
        P=.250 (two-sided)

Table 10g
Off-Diagonal Cells from Table 10a, 10b, 10c, and Table 10d for Fisher's
Exact Test

	12 and 13 Year Olds	14 and 15 Year Olds
Abused= delinquent/non-abused=not delinquent	p+- 2	p+- 8
Abused=not delinquent/ not abused=delinquent	p-+ 2	p-+ 0

Fisher's Exact Test*	(Left)	0.091
	(Right)	1.000
	(2-Tail)	0.091

* To run Fisher's test 12 and 13 year olds have been combined to compare
with 14 and 15 years olds combined.

Tables 10-10g show that delinquency referral rates differ by age between abused and non-abused groups in the hypothesized direction. When we compare the fourteen year old abused with controls using the binomial approach we find the p-value = .062. When the fifteen years old abused are compared with controls we find the p-value = .250. To run Fisher's exact test, twelve and thirteen year olds are combined to create a category of young children and fourteen and fifteen year olds are combined to create a category of old children. Fisher's exact test for this comparison yields a p-value of .091. This significance level is within my set significance level. Thus, we reject the null hypothesis of no relationship and accept the research hypothesis as stated.

Although examination of the interaction between race and gender was planned, some empty cells and some small size cells in the contingency table proved it difficult. Thus, the more complex hypothesis of the interaction between race and gender will not be tested.

Within Group Analysis

This section discusses "Within Group Analyses[12]" and presents the results of the hypotheses that examine the variation in delinquency referral rate among the subgroups within the abused population. All of the hypotheses for this section deal with only abused children and there is no variation in abuse, for example, when we examine the variation between males and females, whites and African-Americans, except when we examine the effects of severity. These hypotheses and results are presented below.

A. Basic hypotheses

Hypothesis # 5: Severity: Subjects who have been the victims of severe abuse are hypothesized to have a higher delinquency referral rate than the subjects who experienced less severe abuse.

To test this hypothesis, the abused subjects are divided into two subgroups based on the severity of abuse. There are 170 subjects who are victims of extremely severe abuse and 307 subjects who are victims of lesser levels of severe abuse. As hypothesized, the victims of severe abuse are found to have a higher rate of delinquency referrals compared to the victims of mild abuse. These results are presented in Table 11.

Table 11

Delinquency Among Victims of Severe Abuse and Mild Abuse
Percentages

Total (n=477)	Severe Abuse (n=170)	Mild Abuse (n=307)	Diff-rence	χ^2	P
11.5	14.7	9.8	4.9	2.61	.10

Table 11 shows that the severely abused victims have a higher delinquency referral rate than the victims of mild abuse and this difference is found to be statistically significant at .10 level. Therefore, the null hypothesis of no relationship is rejected and the research hypothesis, as stated is accepted. As discussed the earlier, selected level of significance is the measure of the extent of evidence about H_o and H_a. The smaller the p-value, the more contradictory the data are to H_o because a smaller p-value implies that if H_o were true, it would be unusual to observe data such as those actually observed. The levels of significance determine the probability of Type I (rejecting H_o when it is true) and Type II error (not rejecting H_o when it is false). The smaller the level of significance, the larger the probability of Type II error for a particular alternative value, and vice versa. For this study, we decided to use .10 as the criteria to reject the hypotheses. This increases the probability of Type I error ("false positive" results) (Agresti and Finlay, 1986), yet it is appropriate since the objective is to scan a number of hypotheses to see which might warrant further investigation. From this we can infer that, in general, the context in which the abuse takes place has some effect on the victims' subsequent behavior. Perhaps, the severity of the experience of the incident, contributed to facilitating the learning process and weakening bonds because of the pain and anguish associated with the experience. The victim might have failed to develop any attachment or commitment to the abuser, have any belief in conformity, and felt angry but helpless to do anything, in particular, to the abuser. Engaging in delinquent acts may have provided an avenue to avenge the severe abuse.

Hypothesis # 6: Race: Within the abused population, African-Americans are expected to have a greater delinquency referral rates than whites.

To examine this hypothesis, the abused population is divided into two subgroups: African-Americans and whites and their delinquency referral rates are compared. These results are presented in Table 12.

Table 12
Delinquency Referral Rate Within Abused Subjects by Race
Percentages

Total (n=477)	African-Americans (n=115)	Whites (n=362)	Diff- -rence	χ^2	P
11.5	15.7	0.2	5.5	2.52	.11

Table 12 shows that, as hypothesized, African-Americans have a higher delinquency referral rate than whites. This difference is found to be statistically significant at only the .11 level. Although this level of significance is in close proximity of my set level of significance, I reject my research hypothesis.

> Hypothesis # 7: Gender: Within the abused population, males are expected to have a greater delinquency referral rate than females.

To examine this hypothesis, the abused population is divided into two subgroups by gender and their delinquency referral rates are compared. These results are presented in Table 13.

Table 13.
Delinquency Referral Rate Among Abused Subjects by Gender
Percentages

Total (n=477)	Males (n=176)	Females (n=301)	Diffe- -rence	χ^2	P
11.5	21.0	6.0	15.0	23.6	<.001

Table 13 shows that the delinquency referral rates vary by gender among the abused subjects. Abused males have a higher delinquency referral rate as compared with females. These differences are found to be significant at <.001 level, implying that gender is associated with delinquency significantly.   These are typical findings and are consistent with the delinquency literature, in general, and with the abuse-delinquency literature, in particular, which provide evidence of males having higher likelihood of being involved in delinquency acts. Widom (1989c) found similar differences within the gender subgroups of the abused group population.

These findings are congruous with our conceptualized notions as well. We had conceptualized a lower delinquency referral rate among female subjects due to a differential in socialization norms and expectations. These results support our hypothesized relations. Thus, we reject the null hypothesis of no relationship and accept the research hypothesis as stated.

> Hypothesis # 8: Age: Within the abused population, the older subjects are expected to have a greater delinquency referral rate than the younger subjects.

To examine this hypothesis, the abused population is subdivided into different age subgroups and the delinquency referral rates within these subgroups are compared. These results are presented in Table 14.

Table 14 shows that the delinquency referral rate rises from 4.4% (12 years) to 25% (16 years) with the age. Sixteen year-old subjects have a 82% higher rate than twelve year-old subjects, a 64% higher rate than thirteen year-old subjects, a 44.8% higher rate than fourteen year-old subjects, and a 26.4% higher rate fifteen year-old subjects. These differences between various age groups are found to be statistically significant at the .004 level.   These results are consistent with our hypothesis that there is a linear relationship between age and delinquency. Delinquency rates rise with the increase in age. Thus, I reject the null hypothesis of no relationship and accept the research hypothesis, as stated.

Table 14
Delinquency Referral Rate Among Abused by Age* - Percentages

	Age in Years						
Total (n=477)	12 (n=113)	13 (n=134)	14 (n=130)	15 (n=76)	16 (n=24)	χ	P
11.5	4.4	9.0	13.8	18.4	25.0	14.9	.004

*   Children who were 11+ but not twelve years old yet, have been combined with twelve year old age group.

B. Combined effect hypotheses

Hypotheses 9, 10, and 11 are tested in two ways. Tables 15, 16, and 17 provide general information on the delinquency referral percentages between different groups. Table 18 and Table 18a-18f present the results of logit analysis for interaction hypotheses. These tables present different logistic regression models and examine the fit of those models in explaining the outcome of delinquency.

Hypothesis # 9: Severity-Gender: Within the abused population, the effect of severity is greater for males than for females.

Hypothesis five examined whether the variance in the delinquency referral rate among the subgroups was due to the different degrees of severity within the abused population. The results showed that the severely abused subgroup had a higher delinquency referral rate than the less severely abused subgroup.

Hypothesis seven examined the variance in abused subgroups by gender. The results show that males had higher delinquency referral rate than females. These findings suggest a possibility of an interaction between severity and gender. So, it is hypothesized that the severely abused males will have the highest delinquency referral rate when compared with other subgroups. The abused population is divided into four subgroups. The results of the analysis are presented in Table 15.

Table 15

Delinquency Referral Rate Among the Victims of Severe Abuse and Less Severe Abuse by Gender - Percentages

Male/ Severe (n=92)	Male/less Severe (n=84)	Female/ Severe (n=78)	Female/less Severe (n=223)
19.6	22.6	9.0	4.9

The results presented in Table 15 show that delinquency referral rates differ by the severity of abuse and gender. We find that severely abused males have a higher delinquency referral rate compared to severely abused females. However, we find that severely abused males have a slightly lower delinquency referral rate than less severely abused males. Severely abused females, on the other hand, have a higher delinquency referral rate than less severely abused females. These differences are statistically insignificant, as can be seen form the logistic regression model presented in Table 18c. The coefficient for severity*gender is found to be significant at .18. Thus, the research hypothesis as stated is rejected.

These are atypical findings. Perhaps some of the severely abused males have their self-concepts wounded to an extent that they feel helpless and have no desire to participate in a delinquent act which requires taking initiative and has a potential for further abuse. Cells in each category of these subgroups may also be responsible for the observed differences and levels of significance. We have 92 severely abused males, 84 less severely abused males, 78 severely abused females, and 223 less severely abused females. These relationships need to be explored further.

Hypothesis # 10: Severity-Race: Within the abused population, the effect of severity is greater for African-Americans than for whites.

Hypothesis five examined whether there was any variance in the delinquency referral rate among the subgroups created on the basis of severity within the abused population. The results show that the severely abused subgroup had a higher delinquency referral rate than the less severely abused subgroup. In hypothesis six, we examined the variance in abused subgroups based on racial group. We found that African-Americans had a higher delinquency referral rate than whites. Next, it is hypothesized that the severely abused African-Americans will have the highest delinquency referral rate when compared with other subgroups. The abused population is divided into four subgroups. The results of the analysis are presented in Table 16.

Table 16
Delinquency Referral Rate Among the Victims of Severe Abuse and Less Severe Abuse by Race - Percentages

Afr.-Amer/	Afr.-Am./less Severe	White/ Severe	White/lessSevere Severe
(n=57)	(n=58)	(n=113)	(n=249)
21.1	10.3	11.5	9.6

The results presented in Table 16 are consistent with my hypothesis. I find that the severely abused African-American children have the highest delinquency referral rate when compared with other subgroups. They have a 104% higher delinquency referral rate than less severely abused African-Americans. When these differences are examined further using logistic regression, the results show that the coefficient for severity*race is significant at .32. This level of significance is higher than the set level. Thus, the research hypothesis as stated, is rejected.

Hypothesis # 11: Race-Gender: Within the abused population, the effects of race on delinquency are greater for males than for females.

Hypothesis seven examined the racial-group-abuse relationship and the results indicate that African-Americans suffer a higher impact of abuse in terms of delinquency when compared with whites, even though the difference was not statistically significant. Hypothesis eight examined the gender-abuse relationship and it shows that males suffer a higher impact of abuse in terms of delinquency when compared with females. These findings suggest that if males and African-Americans are the "at-risk" subgroups then racial group and gender combined may explain some of the variance among the subgroups within the abused group population. To examine this, the abused group population is divided into subgroups and the results are presented in Table 17.

Table 17

Delinquency Referral Rate Among Abused Subjects by Racial Group and Gender - Percentages

	Delinquent	Not Delinquent
Race and Gender		
Male		
White (n=138)	20.3	79.7
Afr.-Amer. (n=38)	23.7	76.3
Female		
White (n=224)	4.0	96.0
Afr.-Amer. (n=77)	11.7	88.3

These results show that the abused African-American males have a higher delinquency referral rate than that of the abused white males, the abused white females, and the abused females. Even though these findings are in the general direction of the hypothesis, logistic regression yields a significance level of .147 for gender*race coefficient. This low statistical significance does not allow me to accept the research hypothesis as stated.

As discussed in the procedure section, a logistic regression analysis is utilized to model how the proportion of responses of the dichotomous dependent variable (delinquency referral) depends on independent variables. Six models and six equations are presented. The first model is the main model that tests the effect of all the main independent variables on the dependent variable. Thus, the first equation in the logistic model is: ln(p/1-p) = a + b*severe + b*gender + b*race. This model examines the net relationship of delinquency with severity, race, and gender; the bivariate relationship was already tested in hypotheses six, seven, and eight. The equation examines how being a male, (as opposed to being a female), white, (as opposed of being African-American), and being severely abused (as opposed to less severely abused) increases the probability of becoming delinquent, when one takes these three variables into consideration. The odds ratio indicates the predictability of the hypothesized outcome based on the independent variables in the equation.

The second equation is: ln(p/1-p) = a + b*severe + b*gender. It examines the main effects model with severity and gender but without race in the equation. This model tests hypotheses six and eight further to evaluate severity and gender's contribution in predicting delinquency without considering race as one of the variables in the equation.

The third equation is: ln(p/1-p) = a + b*severe + b*gender + b*severe*gender. This equation examines a model with severity, gender, and the interaction between gender and severity without race. This model tests hypotheses nine further to evaluate the contribution made by severity, gender, and severity*gender in predicting delinquency.

The fourth equation is: ln(p/1-p) = a + b*gender + b*race. This equation examines hypotheses seven and eight beyond bivariate relationships to evaluate the predictability of delinquency by gender and race.

The fifth equation is: ln(p/1-p) = a + b*gender + b*race + b*gender*race. This model tests hypothesis eleven. It tests the contribution made by the main variables gender, and race, and an interaction variable gender*race in predicting delinquency.

The sixth equation is: ln(p/1-p) = a + b* severe+ b*race + b*severe*race. This model examines relationship between delinquency, severity, race, and race*severity and tests hypothesis ten. It tests the contribution made by the main variables gender and race, and an interaction variable gender*race in predicting delinquency. These results are presented in Table 18.

In Table 18, the models and their relative model Chi-square statistic along with the degrees of freedom in each model and the p-values are presented. These reported statistics help us understand the change that occurs when a variable is added or excluded. Tables 18a through 18e show coefficients, standard errors, odds ratios, and significance levels for each of the variables used in five different models.

Table 18 provides values of the model Chi-square statistics for the model that includes all three independent variables (race, gender, severity) as well as models testing sets of two (for example, gender + severity and gender + race) and three interaction models (gender*severity, race*severity, and race*gender). If we compare model one and four, we find that the model Chi-square for these models remains the same, telling us that the variable excluded in this model (severity) does not contribute in predicting the outcome of delinquency. This is evident from model two and three as well.

Table 18
Logit Models for Delinquency Referrals By Race, Gender, and Severity

Model	Model Chi-square	D.F.	P
1 Race + Gender + Severity	27.047	3	.000
2 Gender + Severity	23.79	2	.000
3 Gender + Severity + Gender*Severity	25.49	3	.000
4 Gender + Race	27.04	2	.000
5 Gender + Race + Race*Gender	29.16	3	.000
6 Race + severity + Race*Severity	5.20	3	.157

Table 18a
Logit Estimates: Model 1

Parameter	Coefficient	S.E.	Odds Ratio	Sig.
Constant	-1.479	.263		.000
Race	.605	.328	1.83	.065
Gender	-1.474	.320	.22	.000
Severity	.015	.314	1.01	.959

Table 18b
Logit Estimates: Model 2

Parameter	Coefficient	S.E.	Odds Ratio	Sig.
Constant	-1.279	.233		.000
Gender	-1.406	.315	.24	.000
Severity	-.093	.306	.91	.759

Table 18c
Logit Estimates: Model 3

Parameter	Coefficient	S.E.	Odds Ratio	Sig.
Constant	-1.413	.262		.000
Gender	-.903	.475	.40	.057
Severity	.183	.370	1.20	.619
Severity*Gender	-.825	.624	.43	.185

Table 18d
Logit Estimates: Model 4

Parameter	Coefficient	S.E.	Odds Ratio	Sig.
Constant	-1.471	.205		.000
Gender	-1.469	.308	.23	.000
Race	.602	.321	1.82	.061

Table 18e
Logit Estimates: Model 5

Parameter	Coefficient	S.E.	Odds Ratio	Sig.
Constant	-1.368	.211		.000
Gender	-1.805	.400	.16	.000
Race	.198	.436	1.21	.649
Gender*Race	.952	.657	2.59	.147

Table 18f
Logit Estimates: Model 6

Parameter	Coefficient	S.E.	Odds Ratio	Sig.
Constant	-2.040	.294		.000
Race	.718	.438	2.05	.101
Severity	-0.197	.364	.82	.587
Race*Severity	-0.639	.651	.52	.326

Table 18a shows that the odds for African-Americans to be referred for delinquency are significantly higher form whites. Race is found to be a significant predictor of delinquency with African-Americans having a 1.83 times higher probability of being referred for delinquency than whites. Severity does not seem to have increased the odds of the final outcome of delinquency. The negative sign for the coefficient for gender suggests that the likelihood of delinquency decreases for females, since males are coded as '0' and females as '1'. The odds ratio of .22 suggests that the odds for males to be involved in delinquency are increased by 4.54 times as compared with females. The odds-ratio for severity (1.01) suggests that it has virtually no effect on the outcome. The second equation shows that gender has a significant effect while severity is found to have very weak effects.

Tables 18c and 18d confirm the same predictions, i.e., gender and race are significant variables in predicting delinquent behavior while severity does not have much effect. Gender having an effect on the outcome is consistent with our finding reported in Table 13. Severity is found to have very weak effects net of sex and race, even though the bivariate test (Table 11) showed it to be a significant variable. This finding suggests that perhaps the significance of severity found in the earlier bivariate test was due to its correlation with race or gender. This is an important finding.

To simplify the results, findings are presented in a table form. Table 19 shows the hypotheses that were accepted and those that were not accepted.

The next chapter discusses the results of this study.

Table 19
Summary of the Results

Group value	Hypothesis #	Theme	Accepted	P-
Abused and control	1	Abuse->Delinquency	Yes	.038
	2	Gender Difference	No	
	3	Race Difference	No	
	4	Age Difference	Yes	.091
Abused Population	5	Severity	No	.100
	6	Race	Yes	.065
	7	Gender	Yes	.000
	8	Age	Yes	.004
	9	Severity*Gender	No	
	10	Severity*Race	No	
	11	Race*Gender	No	

Chapter 8

Discussion of the Results

This research has addressed several questions concerning the causal relationship between child abuse and delinquency. Using a prospective design, children between the ages of eleven and sixteen, who had been recorded as abused, were compared with the non-abused controls matched on racial group, gender, age, and approximate SES in terms of their subsequent delinquency involvement. Overall, 10% of those who were abused had delinquency referral records, in comparison with 6.4% of the controls.

This study has also engaged in a descriptive analysis of 477 cases of child abuse recorded in District Three of Florida's DHRS. This descriptive analysis examined the effects of severity of abuse, race, gender, and age on delinquency within this abused group. The abuse-control comparison results are discussed below, followed by a discussion of the descriptive results for the abused group alone.

Discussion of Abuse-control - Comparison Findings

The main hypothesis guiding this research was that child abuse is causally related to delinquency. The comparison between abused children and their matched controls shows that the overall experience of abuse places children at a statistically significant increased risk of subsequently becoming delinquent (P=.038) in the early years of their lives after the abuse occurred.

These findings are consistent with previous prospective longitudinal studies that utilized similar designs (McCord, 1983; Widom, 1989a; Zingraff et al., 1993). To facilitate the comparison of this research's results with the earlier studies Table 20 is prepared.

The studies in Table 20 examined the causal relationship between abuse and delinquency (or crime) by comparing abused and non-abused children. These comparisons illustrate two points: (1) Abuse is causally related with delinquency or crime; (2) The follow-up time affects the results. The fact that in every study, regardless of the length of the follow-up period, abused children have higher delinquency rates confirms the relationship of abuse with delinquency. This relationship is heightened with age. The increased likelihood of delinquency in older abused victims could be the effect of abuse, the aging process, or both combined.

Table 20

Comparison of the Delinquency Rates found in Abused and Non-abused Children in this Study and in Previous Prospective Longitudinal Studies

Study	Delinquency Rate in the Abused Group (%)	Delinquency Rate in the Control Group (%)	Abuse Sample Size (n)	Control Sample Size (n)	Follow-up Period
Widom (1989c)	28.6	21.1	908	667	30 Years
McCord (1983)	20	11	131	101	40 Years
Zingraff et al. (1993)	13.7	9	633	177	3-4 Years
Present Study	10.0	6.4	220	220	2-5 Years

The abuse-control comparison in this study allows us to draw the following inferences:

(1) Abused children are at a significantly higher risk of subsequent delinquency, and age contributes significantly to that risk. This increased risk can be explained using the conceptual framework proposed in chapter three. As learning theorists have suggested, an early exposure to a harsh and punitive parental figure and repeated abuse from a close adult can provide "imitation" models to follow later in life. Additionally, imitation and modeling of the abusive behavior might facilitate identification of the abused person with the abuser. The children might start believing that the observed abusive mode of interaction is an appropriate, or the only appropriate, mode of interaction. Eventually, children might internalize that mode of interaction. These beliefs get deeply instilled in the children's minds with age. Another explanation is to consider that the abused children might have learned that they are worthy of blame and the abuse that victimized them. The internalization of this belief solves the problem of having to blame their parents and attribute injustice to them. Children are not equipped intellectually to articulate these judgements. This results in self-hatred and lower self-esteem, which have been found to be related to self and other destructive behavior of delinquency.

(2) The effect of abuse on delinquency does not vary by race and gender. This suggests that abuse has similar effects on delinquency across all categories of gender and race. This is a very important finding suggesting that abuse affects adversely even those who are found to be otherwise less likely to behave delinquently, such as females.

(3) Contrary to some of the claims of earlier studies, these findings show a more modest difference between the abused and the non-abused in terms of delinquency. This can be explained in three distinct ways.

The first possible explanation is that the differences observed in this study are deflated because of the limitations of this particular sample. Three specific factors -- the small sample size, the short abuse window, and the short follow-up period -- might have resulted in the smaller delinquency rates found here.

Some of the findings are not statistically significant because of the small number of cells when the sample is separated into groups. Thus, some of the null findings of this study, such as the no difference in the effect of abuse on delinquency across the different levels of gender or race, must be taken as tentative and should be explored in larger samples.

The rather short abuse window and the short length of follow-up period, no doubt, contributed towards the small differences found in delinquency rates of this study. Thus, it is perfectly possible that some cases of abuse take longer to manifest their effects. Hence, the small observed differences might increase in longer follow-up studies. Such a study with a larger sample and a longer follow-up period is planned. The behavior of these subjects as adults needs to be studied to get a better understanding of the effects of abuse.

The second possible explanation is that this is the true extent of relationship, i.e., there is a relationship between abuse and delinquency but the differences between the abused and non-abused are not very large. Thus, the earlier studies have inflated differences due to the use of inappropriate designs, methodologies, and analytical techniques. As discussed in chapter two, some of the earlier studies had special unrepresentative samples, had no control groups, and had data collected retrospectively. Those factors might have contributed to finding the larger differences in delinquency rates between abused and non-abused. The use of an appropriate control group, better measures of abuse and delinquency, and the use of a prospective design in this study might have helped to reveal a closer to the truth relationship, which is significant but smaller.

Finally, there are some other general factors that might have contributed to reducing the effects of abuse. For example, the experience of abuse might have prepared abused children for the worst and conditioned them to survive under adverse circumstances. The experience of abuse might have trained them in concealing deeds considered to be delinquent by adults. Consequently, it might have been harder to detect the delinquent behavior compared with non-abused subjects. However, this conditioning may be present in all abuse-related samples and is not specific to this study only.

Another reason might be that the effects of abuse are compounded by the effects of poverty. All subjects from both groups are from low-income homes. The effects of poverty may be as bad as abuse when it comes to delinquency. Thus, abuse added to poverty may produce few, if any, additional effects. For example, we know that poverty has a causal effect on delinquency and by this and other studies we know that abuse has an effect on delinquency too. But none of these studies have used income or SES as an independent variable to compare the abused and non-abused children. Poverty in itself is a form of abuse. Thus, even though the subjects in the control group had not experienced abuse per se, they can be considered to be the victims of abuse through poverty. This conclusion is supported by the conclusion drawn by a similar study conducted recently.

Zingraff et al. (1993) found the differences in overall delinquency between poor and impoverished abused and non-abused children samples to be small (4.7%) but the difference between abused and general population samples to be much larger (8.4). Poverty is a general factor and is relevant to most abuse samples drawn from official records, not just to this study.

Another reason might be that the abused victims suffer more from internalizing than externalizing disorders. Consequently, they lack self-motivation, self-initiative, self-confidence, and ability to take any action that requires active participation. This, again, is a general factor and may be true for most abuse samples.

Yet another possible explanation is that since each study uses a sample, the variable results from study to study may reflect sampling variability.

The crucial consideration is that while the delinquency rates in this study are smaller, the difference between the abused and control groups is larger than most studies. In fact, the abused group 10% delinquency rate is 57% higher than 6.4% of the control group. Zingraff et al.'s study has delinquency rates of 13.7 and 9 percent with a difference of 52%.

In summary, the delinquency rates found in this study must be considered high given that this is a study of an early onset of delinquency. The statistically significant differences abused and non-abused matched control established in no uncertain terms the causal relation between child abuse and delinquency.

Discussion of Within Group Descriptive Findings

In addition to examining the differences between abused and control group subjects, this study examined the differences in delinquency referral rates within the abused group population. First, we examined if the severity of abuse had any relation with the delinquency referral rate. Using a bivariate analysis, we found that the severely abused subjects had a marginally higher delinquency referral rate as compared with less severely abused subjects (p=.10). There was evidence in support of the hypothesis that the severity of abuse is one factor that explains variance in delinquency referral rate within the abused group population. However, when we tested the contribution made by the main variables in predicting the delinquency outcome using the logistic regression, it was found that severity has a very weak effect net of race and gender.

Next, some descriptive analyses were performed to examine the variability within the abused group by gender, race, and age. The bivariate and logistic regression results show that the differences between males and females were significant (p=.001). Race was found to be significant. The logistic regression's main model showed that race was a significant predictor of delinquency (p=065). This finding suggests differential "modeling" and "reinforcement" under different circumstances and different social conditions.

Next, we found age to be associated with delinquency. Older children had higher delinquency referral rates than younger children. Previous research (using official statistics and self-reports), as discussed in chapters two, three, and four, indicates that there is a statistically significant positive relationship between age and the occurrence of delinquent acts, at least throughout the adolescent years (Elliot et al., 1989; Hirschi and Gottfredson, 1983). The older subjects had more time to be involved, detected, and reported as delinquent. The variance in delinquency referral rate might be an outcome of aging process, in general.

Based on these findings we can infer: (1) Gender, race, and age are general predictors of delinquency; (2) Severity of abuse does not have any effect on delinquency net of race and gender.

The next section presents the summary and conclusions of the study followed by the directions for future research.

Chapter 9

Summary, Conclusions, and Suggestions for Future Research

Based on the analysis and the discussion of the results, the following conclusions are suggested.

(1) Abuse is significantly associated with delinquency. As mentioned earlier, this study used a control group that was matched with the test group on several variables. Since significant differences were found between the abused and non-abused groups in this quasi-experimental design, used to control for problems earlier studies had been criticized for, then abuse can be seen as having significant effect on delinquency.

(2) Age of the child at the time of study has a significant effect on the outcome of delinquency. The significant relationship observed between abuse, age, and delinquency is similar to that in other studies.

(3) Gender, race, and age are predictors of delinquency. Within-group analyses, where abuse is constant, show that gender, race, and age are predictors of delinquency. These findings are consistent with earlier delinquency studies.

(4) Severity of abuse has an insignificant effect net of race and gender. The severity of the abuse experience does not significantly affect the outcome. Because of the limitations of the data, we were not able to explore the various dimensions of the abuse circumstances and the mechanisms that might play a significant role in contributing to externalizing as well as internalizing disorders. However, the variance in outcome for severely and less severely abused subjects was examined.

Although this study has utilized a more sophisticated methodological design, the results presented here have their own limitations. This research is based on official records of both the independent (abuse) and dependent variables (delinquency). Generalizing these findings to the cases of different types of abuse should be avoided. For example, these results cannot be generalized to the unreported cases of abuse, especially those handled unofficially by private medical doctors.

In addition, because of the homogeneity of the sample, these results are not generalizable to the cases of abuse in higher SES families.

Suggestions For Future Research

In general, this study confirms the results of the studies that utilized roughly similar designs and methodologies. Delinquency may be an ultimate outcome of abuse, but interim outcomes that exacerbate or mitigate the probability of delinquency need to be examined and understood. It seems that most of the research is concerned with examining the abuse and delinquency relationship, perhaps because delinquency is considered an extreme behavior, potentially hazardous to society. However, it seems that researchers are skipping, and perhaps ignoring, more serious and damaging consequences of abuse. Victims of abuse who suffer from internalizing disorders are as potentially unproductive members of society as those who suffer from externalizing disorders like juvenile delinquency.

To have a comprehensive understanding of the relationship and to be able to devise ways to alleviate the effects of abuse, we need to examine and understand the other more hidden but equally damaging consequences of abuse. Future research should examine these subtleties.

Gender, race, and age differences in the delinquency referrals found in this study need to be examined further. Once we get a clear understanding of the association between abuse and delinquency, the factors that encourage or discourage delinquency, and the differences in outcomes for different genders, races, and age groups, we may be in a better position to understand the dynamics and devise prevention and intervention strategies to help solve the problem.

We also need to understand the factors that contribute to the establishment of a one-way relationship between abuse and delinquency for some of the victims and not others. We need to study the interim outcomes and their contribution towards the ultimate outcome.

Apart from delinquency and crime, abuse may have more subtle effects on victims, which have not been yet explored. For example, females may direct their aggression inwardly and be more vulnerable to suffer depression and undergo psychiatric hospitalization as a consequence of childhood abuse than manifest outward aggression (Widom, 1989c). Outcomes for males and females may differ by the type of abuse suffered. All these more subtle manifestations of abuse need to be studied to have a complete understanding of the phenomena and be able to devise effective ways for helping individual victims.

Finally, we need to study and evaluate the effectiveness of the services provided by state and federal agencies to abuse victims. This will improve our understanding of the abuse-delinquency relationship and the mechanisms that can be used to protect victims from adverse effects and to prevent the further damage that a traumatic experience like abuse can do to the individual in particular and to society in general.

Future research needs to examine in more depth the mechanisms that make some of the victims of abuse and not others get involved in delinquency. What is it about abuse that makes delinquency certain for some victims, but an insignificant outcome for others? We need to understand the factors that may influence the development of the delinquency outcome. Previous knowledge about the relationship between abuse and delinquency has been limited by a number of methodological problems found in those studies. The findings reported here have their own limitations. Designs like this one, that depend on official data, are not adequate for understanding the processes mediating the outcome of events (Cook and Campbell, 1979). To understand "the processes and dynamics, the potential protective factors," and the more subtle manifestations of the consequences of abuse, it is important "to follow these individuals over their entire life histories" (Widom, 1989c). Official records may not have revealed or disclosed previously experienced abuse, especially if these incidents were not reported. To inform our understanding of the consequences of abuse and of these processes and dynamics, it is essential that official data be supplemented by personal interviews conducted with these individuals. It is also important to follow these individuals in their adult lives and examine their criminal records as well as their parental lives to test the 'intergenerational transmission hypothesis'.

Chapter 10

Policy Implications

A cursory look at the overall results of this study might lead some to believe that since there are only moderate differences in the delinquency rates between the abused and non-abused children, policies to control crime through the control of child abuse are not justified. No interpretation of these results could be more erroneous. Thus, the following paragraphs attempt to make explicit what is considered to be some of the correct policy implications of this study.

The conclusion that this study reveals moderate differences between the abused and the non-abused is an inappropriate one. What this study reveals is that abused children have statistically significant higher rates of delinquency referral rates as compared with non-abused children even at very early age.

This study examined only the early onset of delinquency as a result of abuse. The subjects in the study are between the ages of eleven and sixteen. The majority of the subjects are thirteen years old. The follow-up period and abuse-window studied are short. The statistically significant differences among children at such a young age, after such a short follow-up period, are a cause for alarm.

These young abused children, as they grow, are likely to be seriously affected by abuse. If abuse has a significant effect on delinquency at this age, then there is reason to be concerned. It is more likely that the effects of abuse will be even more significant at a more advanced age when more risk factors converge on the abused.

Children used for the study in both abused and non-abused groups are from the population that represents lower SES. The moderate difference in their delinquency rates is attributable, in part, to the fact that poverty is a form of abuse. Many social scientists postulate that poverty is associated with crime and delinquency (Shaw and McKay, 1972; Henry and Short, 1954; Glaser and Rice, 1959; Wolfgang and Ferracuti, 1967; Durham, 1988). "The lower-class environment provides limited positive role models for either male or female youths" (Balkan et al., 1980). However, in our society, poverty is seldom seen as a form of abuse. Consequently, impoverished children are neglected by their parents who can not provide for them and by the government who fails to assist them in situations of risk.

The idea that economic deprivation is associated with delinquency and crime is relevant to this study. Children in both groups share the same SES. This suggests that the comparison group children are the victims of abuse through poverty. Many such impoverished children grow up being very bitter and angry. Their delinquent behavior may be an outcome of a life of deprivation.

The officially substantiated abused children have a slightly higher rate of delinquency as compared with non- abused impoverished children because while the abused children might have become delinquent because of abuse and poverty, the impoverished children might have become suspectible to delinquency through poverty also. Since both groups were from the population that is more exposed to the correlates of delinquency, the smaller differences are not a surprise. Policies to deal with child abuse traditionally focus on prevention and intervention. Preventive policies may arrest the problem before it triggers. For example, programs providing help to poor parents who are unable to cater to the needs of their children might prevent situations that precipitate abuse. Such programs might work as shock absorbers in discouraging and preventing delinquency.

In cases, where children have already been abused, intervention programs might help by providing support for the child and perhaps negating the damage caused by a traumatic experience of abuse. Such programs may be quite effective in extenuating the effects of abuse. Results of this study are intended to be seen from this perspective.

The fact that child abuse can have such a significant early onset effect on delinquency is a cause for alarm. The results of this study indicate that abuse has a significant causal effect on delinquency. Policies designed to break the causal effect should be an urgent priority. The prevention and intervention tasks carried out by DHRS should be reinforced with an eye for breaking the vicious cycle of family and social violence that this study has uncovered.

Endnotes

1.In fact none of the concepts presented in the conceptual framework are in this study. However, chalking out this framework is significant for thinking through the issues.

2. FPSS abuse registry has been computerized since 1988 and that determines the temporal limit of population of children in this study.

3. Dependency cases refer to the cases where a child is found by the court to be: abandoned, abused, or neglected by the parents or custodians; surrendered for the purpose of adoption; when parents have failed to substantially comply with the requirements of performance agreement or to be at risk of imminent abuse or neglect by parents or custodian.

4. Reference to the other possible perpetrators than parents is made because HRS code form (CI1652) has all those categories. In actual fact in this study, in all cases the perpetrator was either parent or an adult trusted family member.

5. National Incidence Study is a population self-report and, strictly speaking, figures may be inflated. However, the study provides basic information on the characteristics of abused children.

6. Since HRS computerized data in 1988, we only had access to cases of abuse that was reported and verified in 1988 not prior to 1988. Consequently children born in 1977 actually had only a few months to be reported for abuse, depending upon their date of birth.

7. Age in DHRS records is recorded as the year and the number of days passed in that year. For example, the date of birth for a child born on January 1, 1978 is recorded as 1978001.

8. However, such an analysis is planned for the second wave of this study. For the purposes of this study, delinquency referral is used to measure the subjects' involvement in delinquency. Disposition of the case and response of the state social services agencies is not utilized or analyzed in this study.

9. Eleven and half year Olds are combined with twelve year Olds because there are only a few of eleven and half years old subjects; and sixteen year Olds have been combined with fifteen year Olds for the same reasons.

10. Severe abuse is operationalized based on the injury, as describe
d under the "operationalization of the major constructs." Severity of abuse is measured by the actual physical harm incurred not the number of times abuse occurred.

11. A referral means the subject was referred for delinquent action. A referral could mean just one referral or more than one referral. If there was any record, it was used as a measure of delinquency. At the present stage, no distinction is made between one or more than one delinquency referral.

12. Total delinquency rate among the abused population is 11.5%.

APPENDIX A
LIST OF COUNTIES

01	Alachua
02	Bradford
03	Citrus
04	Columbia
05	Dixie
06	Gilchrist
07	Hamilton
08	Hernando
09	Hillsbrough
10	Lafayette
11	Lake
12	Levy
13	Marion
14	Nassau
15	Pasco
16	Putnam
17	Sumter
18	Suwanne
19	Union

APPENDIX B
LIST OF SERVICES RECEIVED BY THE CONTROL GROUP
CHILDREN

07	Specialized Family Services
09	Local Services Program
11	Family Shelter
12	Non-Family Shelter
13	Crisis Homes
73	Child Day Care
75	Refugee and Entrant Social Services

Adapted from HRS Children, Youth And Families Client Information System.

APPENDIX C
CODE OF DELINQUENCY REFERRALS

Delinquency Referrals

Felonies

01	Murder/Non-negligent Manslaughter
02	Negligent Manslaughter
03	Sexual Battery
04	Other Sex Offenses
05	Armed Robbery
06	Other Robbery
07	Arson
08	Burglary (Breaking and Entering)
09	Auto Theft
10	Grand Larceny
11	Receiving Stolen Property over $100
12	Concealed Firearm
13	Aggravated Assault and/or Battery
14	Forgery
15	Felony Violation of Drug Laws
16	Felony Marijuana Offense
17	Escape From Training School
18	Resisting Arrest With Violence
19	Shooting/Throwing a Deadly Missile into Occupied Dwelling/Vehicle
20	Other Felony

Misdemeanors

21	Assault and/or Battery (not aggravated)
22	Prostitution
23	Sex Offenses not Included in 03, 04, or 22
24	Petit Larceny (excluding Retail Theft)
25	Retail Theft (Shoplifting)
26	Receiving Stolen Property
27	Concealed Weapon (Except Firearms)
28	Disorderly Conduct
29	Criminal Mischief (Vandalism)
30	Trespassing
31	Loitering and Prowling
32	Misdemeanor Violation of Drug Laws

(Excluding Marijuana)

33	Misdemeanor Marijuana Offense
34	Possession of Alcohol Beverages
35	Other Alcohol Offenses
36	Violation of Hunting, Fishing, and Boating Laws
37	Resisting Arrest Without Violence
38	Unauthorized Use of Motor Vehicle
39	Other Misdemeanor

Other Delinquency

40	Contempt of Court
41	Violation of County or Municipal Ordinance
42	Felony Traffic Offense (Including Leaving the Scene of an Accident Involving Death or Personal Injury)
43	Other Traffic Offenses

Status Offenses

80	Local Runaway
81	Runaway From Other Florida County
82	Out-of-State Runaway
83	Truancy
84	Beyond Control

Adapted from HRS Children, Youth And Families Client Information System Form (50-4).

APPENDIX D
DEFINITION OF ABUSE

Florida Protection from Abuse, Neglect, and Exploitation, defines an abused or neglected child as:

> A child whose physical or mental health or welfare is harmed, or threatened with harm, by the acts or omissions of the parent or other person responsible for the child's welfare or for purposes of reporting requirements, by any person.

> A child means any person under the age of 18 years.

"Harm" to a child's health or welfare can occur when the parent or other person responsible for the child's welfare:

(a)   Inflicts, or allows to be inflicted, upon the child physical or mental injury.

        Such injury includes, but is not limited to:

1.   Injury sustained as a result of excessive corporal punishment;

(b)   Commits, or allows to be committed, sexual battery, as defined in Chapter 794, against the child or commits, or allows to be committed, sexual abuse of a child;

©   Exploits a child, or allows a child to be exploited, as provided in s. 450.151;

(d)   Abandons the child;

(e)   Fails to provide the child with supervision or guardianship by specific acts or omissions of a serious nature requiring the intervention of the department or the court;

(f)   Fails to supply the child with adequate food, clothing, shelter, or health care, although offered financial or other means to do so.

        [s. 415.503,F.S.]

APPENDIX E
CODE OF INJURIES SUSTAINED DURING ABUSE

Physical Injuries

01	Bruises/Welts
02	Cuts/Punctures/Wounds/Bite Marks
03	Burns/Scalds
05	Sprain/Dislocation
06	Bone Fractures
10	Internal Injuries
11	Skull Fracture/Brain Damage/Subdural Hematoma
13	Asphyxiation/Suffocation/Drowning
18	Excessive Corporal Punishment
19	Other Physical Injury

Sexual Injuries

20	Sexual Battery-Incest
21	Sexual Battery-Not Incest
24	Sexual Molestation
25	Sexual Exploitation
29	Other Sexual Abuse

Mental Injury

31	Harassed, Belittled, or Ridiculed
33	Inappropriate or Excessive Use of Restraints
35	Inappropriate or Excessive Use of Isolation
37	Confinement/Bizarre Punishment
39	Other Mental Injury

Lack of Supervision

50	Inadequate Supervision-Parent Present
51	Inadequate Supervision-Parent Not Present
52	Inadequate Supervision-Lockout
53	Abandonment

Environmental Neglect

55	Conditions Hazardous to Health
56	Inadequate Shelter
57	Inadequate Clothing
58	Inadequate Food

Lack of Health Care

60	Malnutrition
61	Failure to Thrive
63	Failure to Provide Medical Care for Religious Reasons
65	Medical Neglect

Adapted from HRS Florida Protective Services System: Victim/Child Screen (CII632).

BIBLIOGRAPHY

Aber, J. and Allen, J. (1987). Effects of maltreatment on young children's socioemotional development: An attachment theory perspective. Developmental Psychology, 23, 406-414.

Aber, J., Allen, J., and Cicchetti, D. (1984). The socio-emotional development of maltreated children: An empirical and theoretical analysis. In H. Fitzgerald, B. Ester, and M. Youngman (Eds.), Theory and Research in Behavioral Pediatrics. New York: Plenum Press.

Aber, J., Allen, J., Carlson, V. and Cicchetti, D. (1989). The effects of maltreatment on development during early childhood: Recent studies and their theoretical, clinical, and policy implications. In D. Cicchetti and V. Carlson (eds.), Child Maltreatment: Theory and Research on the Causes and Consequences of Child Abuse and Neglect. (pp. 579-619). Cambridge: Cambridge University Press.

Aber, J., and Zigler, E. (1981). Developmental considerations in the definition of child maltreatment. In R. Rizely and D. Cicchetti (eds.), Developmental Perspectives on Child Maltreatment, Vol. 11. New Directions for Child Development, (pp. 1-31). San Francisco: Jossey-Bass.

Agresti, A. and Finlay, B. (1986). Statistical Methods for the Social Sciences. (2nd edition). Collier Macmillian Publishers. London, Division of Macmillian, Inc.

Ainsworth, M. and Witting, B. (1969). Attachment and exploratory behavior of one-year-Olds in a strange situation. In B. Foss (eds.), Determinants of infant behavior: Vol. 4, (pp. 113-136). London: Methuen.

Akers, R. L. (1985). Deviant Behavior: A Social Learning Approach (3rd edition). Belmont, CA: Wadsworth Publishing Company.

Alfaro, J. (1981). Report on the relationship between child abuse and neglect and later socially deviant behavior. In R. Hunner and Y. Walker (eds.), Exploring the Relationship Between Child Abuse and Delinquency. Montclair, NJ: Allanheld, Osmun.

Altemeier, W. A., Vietze, P. M., Sherrod, K. B., Sandler, H., Falsey, S. and O'Connor, S. (1979). Prediction of child maltreatment during pregnancy. Journal of American Academy Child Psychiatry, 18, 205-218.

Alvy, K.T. (1975) Preventing child abuse. American Psychologist, 30 ,21- 928.

Ammerman, T. R. and Hersen, M. (1990). Research in child abuse and neglect: Current status and an agenda for the future. In R. Ammerman and M. Hersen (eds.), Children at Risk (pp. 3-22). New York: Plenum.

Aragona, J.A. and Eyberg, S. M. (1981). Neglected children: Mothers' report of child behavior problems and observed verbal behavior. Child Development, 52, 596-602.

Azar, S.T., Barnes, K.T., and Twentyman, C.T. (1988). Developmental

outcomes in physically abused children: Consequences of parental abuse or the effects of a more general breakdown in care giving behaviors? Behavior Therapist, 11, 27-32.

Balkan, S., Berger, R., and Schmidt, J. (1980) Crime and Deviance in America: A Critical Approach. Wadsworth Publishing Company. Belmont, CA.

Bandura, A. (1973). Aggression: A Social Learning Analysis. Englewood Cliffs, NJ: Prentice-Hall.

Bandura, A. (1977). Social Learning Theory. Englewood Cliffs, NJ: Prentice- Hall.

Besharov, D. J. (1982). Toward better research on child abuse and neglect: Making definitional issues an explicit concern. Child Abuse and Neglect, 5, 383-390.

Besharov, D. J. (1983). Child abuse: Past progress, present problems, and future directions. Family Law Quarterly, 17, 151-172.

Besharov, D. J. (1984). Protecting abused and neglected children: Can law and social work help? In W. Holder and K. Hayes (eds.), Malpractice and Liability in Child Protective Services (pp. 29-48). Longmont, CA:Bookmakers Guild.

Blount, H.R. and Chandler, T.A. (1979). Relationship between childhood abuse and assaultive behavior in adolescent male psychiatric patients. Psychology Reports, 44, 1126.

Bolton, F.G., Reich, J. and Guiterres, S.E. (1977). Delinquency patterns in maltreated children and siblings. Victimology, 2, 349-359.

Boshua, D.M, and Twentyman, C.T. (1984). Mother-child interactional style in abuse, neglect, and control groups: naturalistic observations in the home. Journal of Abnormal Psychology, 93, 106-114.

Brown, A. and Finkelhor, D. (1986). Impact of child sexual abuse: A review of research. Psychological Bulletin , 99, 66-77.

Burgess, A. W., Hartman, C. R., and McCormack, A. (1987). Abused to abuser: Antecedents of socially deviant behaviors. American Journal of Psychiatry, 144, 1431-1436.

Burgess, R.L. and Conger, R.D. (1978). Family interaction in abusive, neglectful, and normal families. Child Development, 49, 1163-1173.

Campbell, T.D. and Stanley C.J. (1963). Experimental and Quasi-experimental Designs for Research. Rand McNally and Company: Chicago.

Carlson, V., Cicchetti, D., Barnett, D. and Braunwald, K. (1989). Finding order in disorganization: Lessons from research on maltreated infants' attachments to their care-givers. In Cicchetti, D.and Carlson, V. (eds.) Child Maltreatment: Theory and Research on the Causes and Consequences of Child Abuse and Neglect (pp. 579-619). Cambridge: Cambridge University Press.

Cicchetti, D. (1984). The emergence of developmental psychopathology. Child Development, 55, 1-7.

Cicchetti, D. and Barnett D. (1991). Toward the development of a scientific nosology of child maltreatment. In Dante Cicchetti and William Grove (eds.), Thinking Clearly about Psychology. Minneapolis: University of Minnesota Press.

Cicchetti, D., and Carlson, V. (1989). Child Maltreatment: Theory and Research on the Causes and Consequences of Child Abuse and Neglect (pp. 579-619). Cambridge: Cambridge University Press.

Cicchetti, D., and Rizley, R. (1981). Developmental perspectives on the etiology, intergenerational transmission and sequelae of child maltreatment. New Directions for Child Development, 11, 31-55.

Cicchetti, D., and Sroufe, L. A. (1976). The relationship between affective and cognitive development in Down's Syndrome infants. Child Development, 47, 920-929.

Climent, C., and Ervin, F.R. (1972). Historical data in the evaluation of violent subjects: a hypothesis generating study. American Journal of Psychiatry, 27, 621-624.

Conway, L. P., and Hensen, D. J. (1989). Social behavior of physically abused and neglected children: A critical review. Clinical Psychology Review, 9, 627-652.

Cook, D.T. and Campbell T.D. (1979). Quasi-Experimentation Design and Analysis Issues for Field Settings. Houghton Mifflin Company. Boston.

Crittenden, P.M. (1985). Maltreated infants: Vulnerability and resilience. Journal of Child Psychology and Psychiatry, 26, 85-96.

Crittenden, P.M. (1988). Relationships at risk. In J. Belsky and T. Nezworski (eds.), Clinical Implications of Attachment Theory (pp. 136-174). Hillsdale, NJ: Erlbaum.

Curtis, G.C. (1963). Violence breeds violence-perhaps? American Journal of Psychiatry, 120, 386-387.

Daro, D. (1988). Confronting Child Abuse. New York: Free Press.

Dean, A.L., Malik, M., Richards, W., and Stringer, S.A. (1986). Effects of parental maltreatment on children's conceptions of interpersonal relationships. Developmental Psychology, 22, 617-626.

Duncan, J. W., and Duncan, J.M. (1971). Murder in the family: A study of homicidal adolescents. American Journal of Psychiatry, 127, 74-79.

Durham, A. M., III (1988). Ivy league delinquency: a self-report analysis. American Journal of Criminal Justice, 12, 167-197.

Eason, W.M., and Steinhilber, R.M. (1961). Murderous aggression by children and adolescents. Archives of General Psychiatry, 4, 27-35.

Egeland, B. and Brunnquell, D. (1979). An at-risk approach to the study of child abuse. Journal of the American Academy of Child Psychiatry, 18, 219-236.

Egeland, B. and Sroufe, A. (1981a). Attachment and early maltreatment. Child Development, 52, 44-52.

Egeland, B. and Sroufe, A. (1981b). Developmental sequelae of maltreatment in infancy. In R. Rizely and D. Cicchetti (eds.) Developmental Perspectives on Child Maltreatment, Vol. 11, New directions for Child Development (pp. 77-92). San Francisco: Jossey-Bass.

Egeland, B. and Sroufe, A. and Erickson, M. (1983). The developmental consequences of different patterns of maltreatment. Child Abuse and Neglect, 7, 459-469.

Elliott, D.S., David H., and Scott M. (1989). Multiple Problem Youth: Delinquency, Substance Abuse, and Mental Health Problems. New York: Springer-Verlag.

Elmer, E. (1977). Children in Jeopardy: A Study of Abused Minors and Families. University of Pittsburgh Press.

Elmer, E. and Gregg, G.S. (1967). Developmental characteristics of abused children. Pediatrics, 40, 596-602.

Erickson, M.F., Egeland, B., and Pianta, R. (1989). The effects of maltreatment on the development of young children. In D. Cicchetti and V. Carlson (eds.), Child Maltreatment, (pp.647-684). Cambridge: Cambridge University Press.

Eyeberg, S. M., and Ross, A. W. (1978). Assessment of child behavior problems: the validation of a new inventory. Journal of Clinical Child Psychology, 7, 107-126.

Farrington, D. (1978). The family backgrounds of aggressive youths. In L. Hershov and M. Berger (eds.), Aggression and Antisocial Behavior in Childhood and Adolescence. Book supplement to Journal of Child Psychology and Psychiatry, No. 1. New York: Pergamon.

Finkelhor, D. and Hotalling, G. T. (1984). Sexual abuse in the national incidence study of child abuse and neglect: An appraisal. Child Abuse and Neglect, 8, 23-33.

Friedman, S. and Morse, C. W. (1974). Child abuse: A five year follow up of early case findings in the emergency department. Pediatrics, 54, 404-410.

Friedreich, W.H., Einbender, A. J., and Luecke, W. J. (1983). Cognitive and behavioral characteristics of physically abused children. Journal of Consulting and Clinical Psychology, 51, 313-314.

Garbarino, J. (1976). A preliminary study of some ecological correlates of child abuse: The impact of socioeconomic stress on mothers. Child Development, 47, 178-185.

Garbarino, J. (1989). The incidence and prevalence of child maltreatment. In L. Ohlin and M. Tonry (eds.), Family Violence, (pp. 219-262). Chicago: University of Chicago Press.

Garbarino, J. (1990). Future directions. In R. Ammerman and M. Hersen (eds.), Children At Risk, (p. 291-297).

Garbarino, J. and Gilliam, G. (1980). Understanding Abusive Families. Lexington, MA: Lexington Books.

Garbarino, J., and Plantz, M. (1986). Child abuse and Juvenile delinquency: What are the links? In J. Garbarino, C. Schellenbach, and J. Sebes (eds.) Troubled Youth, Troubled Families, (pp. 27-39). New York: Aldine.

Geller, M. and Ford-Somma, L. (1984). Violent Homes, Violent Children: A Study of Violence in the Families of Juvenile Offenders (prepared for the National Center on Child Abuse and Neglect). Trenton: New Jersy State Department of Corrections, Division of Juvenile Services.

Gelles, R. (1973). Child abuse as psychopathology: A sociological critique and reformulation. American Journal of Orthopsychiatry, 43, 611-621.

Gelles, R. J. (1980). Violence in the family. A review of research in the seventies. Journal of Marriage and Family, 42, 873-885.

Gelles, R.J., and Straus, M.A. (1987). Is violence toward children increasing? A comparison of 1975 and 1985 national survey rates. Journal of Interpersonal Violence, 2, 212-222.

George, C. and Main, M. (1979). Social interactions of young abused children: Approach, avoidance, and aggression. Child Development, 50, 306-318.

Gil, D. (1973). Violence against children: Physical child abuse in the United States. Cambridge MA: Harvard University Press.

Glaser, D. and Rice, K. (1959). Crime, age, and employment. American Sociological Review, 24, 5.

Glasgow, D. (1981). The Black Underclass. (New York: Vintage Books).

Glueck, S. and Glueck, E. (1950). Unravelling Juvenile Delinquency. Cambridge: Cambridge University Press.

Green, A. (1978). Psychopathology of abused children. Journal of the American Academy of Child Psychiatry, 17, 92-103.

Groeneveld, L. P. and Giovannoni, J. M. (1977). Disposition of child abuse and neglect cases. Social Work Research and Abstracts, 13, 24-30.

Gutierres, S. and Reich, J. A. (1981). A developmental perspective on runaway behavior: Its relationship to child abuse. Child Welfare, 60, 89-94.

Hartstone, E. and Hansen, K. V. (1984). The violent crime juvenile offender: an empirical portrait, In Mathias, Demuro, and Allinson (eds.), Violent Juvenile Offenders: An Anthology. San Francisco: National Council on Crime and Delinquency.

Henry, A. F. and Short, F. S. (1954). Suicide, and Homicide: Some Economic, Sociological, and Psychological Aspects of Aggression. New York: Free Press.

Hershorn, M., and Rosenbaum, A. (1985). Children of marital violence: A closer look at the unintended victims. American Journal of Orthopsychiatry, 55, 260-266.

Hindelang, M. J., Hirschi, T. and Weis, J. (1981). Measuring Delinquency. Beverely Hills, CA: Sage.

Hirschi, T. (1969). Causes of Delinquency. Berkeley: University of California Press.

Hirschi, T., and M. Gottfredson (1983). Age and explanation of crime. American Journal of Sociology, 89, 552-584.

Hoffman-Plotkin, D., and Twentyman, C. (1984). A multi-model assessment of behavioral and cognitive deficits in abused and neglected preschoolers. Child Development, 55, 794-802.

Hotalling, G., Straus, M., and A. Lincoln. (1989). Interfamily violence, and crime and violence outside the family. In L. Ohlin and M. Tonry (eds.) Family Violence, 315-376. Chicago: University of Chicago.

Hughes, H. M., Parkinson, D., and Vargo, M. (1989). Witnessing spouse abuse and experiencing physical abuse: A "double whammy"? Journal of Family Violence, 4, 197-209.

Jaffee, P., Wolfe, D.A., Wilson, S. and Zak, L. (1986). Similarities in behavioral and social maladjustment among child victims and witnesses to family violence. American Journal of Orthopsychiatry, 56, 142-146.

Jenkins, R. L. (1968). The varieties of children's behavioral problems and family dynamics. American Journal of Psychiatry, 124, 1440-1445.

Justice, B., and Justice, R. (1976). The Abusing Family. New York: Human Services Press.

Kaufman, J., and Cicchetti, D. (1989). The effects of maltreatment on school-aged children's socioemotional development. Developmental Psychology, 25, 375-487.

Kaufman, J., and Zigler, E. (1987). Do abused children become abusive parents? American Journal of Orthopsychiatry, 57, 186-192.

Kazdin, A., Moser, J., Colbus, D., and Bell, R. (1985). Depressive symptoms among physically abused and psychiatrically disturbed children. Journal of Abnormal Psychology, 94, 298-307.

Kempe, C.H., Silverman, F.N., Steele, B.F., Droegemueller, C.J.,and Silver H.K. (1962). The battered child syndrome. Journal of American Medical Association, 181, 105-112.

Kinard, E. (1980). Emotional development in physically abused children. American Journal of Orthopsychiatry, 50, 686-696.

King, C.H. (1975). The ego and the integration of violence in homicidal youth. American Journal of Orthopsychiatry, 50, 686-696.

Klimes-Dougan, B. Kistner, J. (1990). Physically abused preschoolers' responses to peers' distress. Developmental Psychology, 26, 599-602.

Kotelchuck, M. (1982). Child abuse and neglect: prediction and misclassification. In R. H. Starr Jr. (ed.), Child abuse Prediction. Cambridge, MA: Ballinger.

Kratcoski, P.C. (1982). Child abuse and violence against the family. Child Welfare, 61, 435-444.

Kratcoski, P.C. (1985). Youth violence directed toward significant others. Journal of Adolescence, 8, 145-157.

Leventhal, J.M. (1982). Research strategies and methodologic standards in studies of risk factors for child abuse. Child Abuse and Neglect, 6, 113-123.

Lewis, D., Mallough, C., and Webb, V. (1989). Child abuse, delinquency, and violent criminality. In D. Cicchetti and V. Carlson (eds.) Child Maltreatment: Theory and Research on the Causes and Consequences of Child Abuse and Neglect, (pp. 707-721). Cambridge: Cambridge University Press.

Lewis, D., and Shanok, S. (1977). Medical histories of delinquent and nondelinquent children: An epidemiological study. American Journal of Psychiatry, 134, 1020-1025.

Lewis, D., Shanok, S., Pincus, J., and Glaser, G. (1979). Violent juvenile delinquents: Psychiatric, neurological, psychological, and abuse factors. Journal of the American Academy of Child Psychiatry, 18, 307-319.

Lewis, D.O., Moy, E., Jackson, R. Restifo, N., Serra, S., and Simos A. (1985). Biopsychological characteristics of children who later murder: a prospective study. American Journal of Psychiatry, 142, 1161-1167.

Loeber, R. and Dishion, J.T. (1983). Early predictors of male adolescent delinquency: A review. Psychological Bulletin, 94, 68-99.

Lynch, M. A. and Roberts, J. (1982). Consequences of Child Abuse. London: Academic Press.

Main, M., and George, C. (1985). Responses of abused and disadvantaged toddlers to distress in age mates: A study in the day care setting. Developmental Psychology, 21, 407-412.

Martin, H. P. (1976). The Abused Child. Cambridge, MA: Ballinger.

Martin, H.P. and Beezeley, P. (1977). Behavioral observations of abused children. Developmental Medicine and Child Neurology, 19, 373-387.

Mash, E. and Wolfe, A.D. (1991). Methodological issues in research on physical abuse. Criminal Justice and Behavior, 8, 8-29.

Mayall, P.D., and Norgard, K.E. (1983). Child Abuse and Neglect: Sharing Responsibility. New York: John Wiley and Sons.

McCord, J. (1983). A forty-year perspective on effects of child abuse and neglect. Child Abuse and Neglect, 7, 265-270.

McCord, J. (1986). Instigation and insulation: How families affect antisocial aggression. In D. Olewus, J. Block, and M. Radke-Yarrow (eds.), Development of Antisocial and Prosocial Behavior, (pp. 343-357). New York: Academic Press.

McCormack, A., Mark-David, J. and Burgess, A. W. (1986). Runaway youths and sexual victimization: Gender differences in an adolescent runaway population. Child Abuse and Neglect, 10, 387-395.

Merton, R. K. (1968). Social Theory and Social Structure. New York: Free Press.

Monane, M., Leichter, D. and Lewis, D.O. (1984). Physical abuse in psychiatrically hospitalized children and adolescents. Journal of the American Academy of Child Psychiatry, 23, 653-658.

Morgan, S. R. (1987). Psycho-educational profile of emotionally disturbed abused children. Journal of Clinical Child Psychology, 8, 3-6.

Morse, C.W., Sahler, O.J. and Friedman, S.B. (1970). A three-year follow-up study of abused and neglected children. American Journal of Diseases of Children, 120, 439-446.

Mouzakitis, C.M. (1981). An inquiry into the problem of child abuse and juvenile delinquency. In Hunner and Walker (eds.) Exploring the Relationship between Child Abuse and Delinquency, (pp. 220-232). Montclair, NJ: Allanheld, Osmun.

Mueller, E. and Silverman, N. (1991). Peer relations in maltreated children. In Dante Cicchetti and Vicki Carlson (eds.), Child Maltreatment: Theory and Research on the Causes and Consequences of Child Abuse and Neglect. New York: Cambridge Press.

Neapolitan-Jerry (1981) Parental influences on aggressive behavior: A social learning approach. Adolescence, 64, 831-840.

Newberger, E.H., Newberger, M., and Hampton R. (1983). Child abuse: the current theory base and future research needs. Journal of the American Academy of Child Psychiatry, 22, 262-268.

Newberger, E.H., Reed, R.B., Daniel, J. H., Hyde, J. N., and Kotelchuck, M. (1977). Pediatric social illness: Towards an etiological classification. Pediatrics, 50, 178-185.

Oates, R.K., and Peacock, A. (1985). Intellectual development of battered children. Australia and New Zealand Journal of Developmental Disabilities, 10, 27-29.

Olweus, D. (1980). Familial and temperamental determinants of aggressive behavior in adolescent boys: a causal analysis. Developmental Psychology, 16, 644-660.

Oliver, J.E. and Taylor, A. (1971). Five generations of ill-treated children in one family pedigree. British Journal of Psychiatry, 119, 473-480.

Otto, K. R. and Melton, B.G. (1991) Trends in legislation and case law on child abuse and neglect. In Ammerman and Hersen (eds.), Children At Risk: An Evaluation of Factors Contributing to Child Abuse and Neglect. (p.55-84) Plenum Press.

Patterson, G. R. (1976). The aggressive child: Victim and architect of a coercive system. In E. Mash, L. Hammerlynck, and L. Handy (eds.), Behavior Modification and Families (pp. 267-316). New York; Brunner/Mazel.

Patterson, G.R. (1979). A performance theory for coercive family interaction. In R. B. Cairns (eds.), The Analysis of Social Interactions: Method, Issues, and Illustrations (pp. 117-162). Hillsdale, NJ : Erlbaum.

Patterson, G.R. (1982). Coercive Family Process. Eugene, Or: Castalia.

Patterson, G.R., Reid, J.B., Jones, R.R., and Conger, R. (1975). A Social Learning Approach to Family Intervention, 1, Eugene, OR: Castalia.

Pelton, L. H. (1978). Child abuse and neglect: The myth of classlessness. American Journal of Orthopsychiatry, 48, 608-617.

Perry, M., Wells, E., and Doran, L. (1983). Parent characteristics in abusing and nonabusing families. Journal of Clinical Child Psychology, 12, 329-336.

Pianta, R., Byron, E. and Martha, F. E. (1989). The antecedents of maltreatment: Results from the mother-child interaction research project. In Dante Cicchetti and Vicki Carlson (eds.), Child Maltreatment: Theory and Research on the Causes and Consequences of Child Abuse and Neglect. New York: Cambridge University Press.

Plotkin, R. C., Azar, S. Twentyman, C. T., and Perri, M. G. (1981). A critical evaluation of the research methodology employed in the investigation of causative factors of child abuse and neglect. Child Abuse and Neglect, 5, 449-455.

Reidy, T.J. (1977). The aggressive characteristics of abused and neglected children. Journal of Clinical Psychology, 33, 1140-1145.

Ressler, R.K. and Burgess, A.W. (1985). The men who murdered. FBI Law Enforcement Bulletin, 54, 2-6.

Rosenberg, M.S. (1987). Children of battered women: The effects of witnessing violence on their social problem-solving abilities. Behavior Therapist, 4, 85-89.

Schulsinger, F. , Sarnoff. A. M., and Kopp J. (1981) Longitudinal Research: Methods and Uses in Behavioral Sciences. Boston: Matinus Nijhoff.

Sendi, I.B. and Blomgren, P.G. (1975). A comparative study of predictive criteria in the predisposition of homicidal adolescents. American Journal of Psychiatry, 132, 423-427.

Shaw, C. R. and McKay, H. D. (1972). Juvenile Delinquency and Urban Areas. (rev. ed.). Chicago, IL: University of Chicago Press.

Siegel, S. (1956). Nonparametric Statistics for the Behavioral Sciences. McGraw Hill: New York.

Silver, L.R., Dublin, C.C. and Laurie R.S. (1969). Does violence breed violence? Contributions from a study of the child abuse syndrome. American Journal of Psychiatry, 126, 152-155.

Spinetta, J.J. and Rigler, D. (1972). The child-abusing parent: a psychological review. Psychological Bulletin, 77, 296-304.

Starr, R.H. (1979). Child abuse. American Psychologist, 34, 872-878.

Starr, R.H., Howard, D. and Beverely A. B. (1990). The Epidemiology of child maltreatment. In R. Ammerman and M. Hersen (eds.), Children at Risk. (pp. 23-50). New York: Plenum.

Steele, B.F. (1986). Notes on the lasting effects of early child abuse throughout the life cycle. Child Abuse and Neglect, 10, 283-291.

Steele, B.F. and Pollock, C.B. (1974). A psychiatric study of parents who abuse infants and small children. In R.E. Helfer and C.H. Kempe (eds.), The Battered Child. (pp. 80-133). Chicago: University of Chicago Press.

Stouffer, S. (1962) Social Research to Test Ideas. New York: The Free Press of Glencoe.

Straker, G., and Jacobson, R. (1981) Aggression, emotional maladjustment, and empathy in the abused child. Developmental Psychology, 17, 762-765.

Straus, M. A., Gelles, R., and Steinmetz, K. S. (1980). Behind Closed Doors. New York: Anchor/Doubleday Press.

Tallahassee: State of Florida Governor's Office. Department of Health and Rehabilitative Services (1991). Florida Protective Services System: Annual Report 1991. Governor's Office.

Tarter, R.E., Hegedus, A. M., Winsten, N.E., and A.I. Alterman (1984). Neuropsychological, personality, and familial characteristics of physically abused delinquents. Journal of the American Academy of Child Psychiatry, 23, 668-674.

Tuteur, W., and Glotzer, J. (1966). Further observations on murdering mothers. Journal of Forensic Sciences, 11, 373-383.

Wassermann, G.A. and Allen, R. (1983). Going beyond abuse: maladaptive patterns of interaction in abusing mother-infant pairs. Journal of the American Academy of Child Psychiatry, 22, 245-252.

Wick, S.C. (1981). Child abuse as causation of juvenile delinquency in Central Texas. In R.J. Hunner and Y.E. Walker (eds.), Exploring the Relationship between Child Abuse and Delinquency. Montclair, NJ: Allanheld, Osmun.

Widom, C.S. (1989a). The intergenerational transmission of violence. In Weiner and Wolfgang (eds.), Pathways to Criminal Violence (pp. 137-201).

Widom, C. S. (1989b). Does violence beget violence? A critical examination of the literature. Psychological Bulletin, 106, 3-28.

Widom, C. S. (1989c). Child abuse, neglect, and violent criminal behavior. Criminology, 27, 251-271.

Wilson, B. (1987). The Truly Disadvantaged. Chicago: The University of Chicago Press.

Wolfe, D.A. (1985). Child Abuse: Implications for Child Development and Psychopathology. Newberry Beverely Hills, CA: Sage.

Wolfe, D.A., and Mosk, M.D. (1983). Behavioral comparisons of children from abusive and distressed families. Journal of Consulting and Clinical Psychology, 51, 702-708.

Wolfgang, M. and Ferracuti, F. (1967). <u>The Subculture of Violence: Towards an integerated Theory of Criminology</u>. London: Tavistock.

Youngblade, L. and Belsky, J. (1990). Social and emotional consequences of child maltreatment. In R. Ammerman and M. Hersen (eds.), <u>Children at Risk</u>, (pp. 109-146). New York: Plenum.

Zingraff, T. M., Jeffrey, L., Kristen, A. M., and Mathew C. J. (1993). Child maltreatment and youthful problem behavior. <u>Criminology, 31</u>(2), 172-202.

Index

Suman Kakar, Ph.D., is Assistant Professor of Criminal Justice at the Florida International University, Miami. Dr. Kakar earned her under-graduate degree in Political Science and master's in Economics from the Punjab University in India. She earned her doctorate from the University of Florida. Her research focuses on child abuse, domestic violence, and juveniles.